VOLUME 2 • SOUTHERN CALIFORNIA

Camper's Guide to CALIFORNIA

Parks, Lakes, Forests, and Beaches

Where to Go and How to Get There

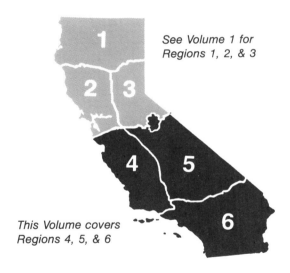

See Volume 1 for
Regions 1, 2, & 3

This Volume covers
Regions 4, 5, & 6

Mickey Little

Gulf Publishing Company

VOLUME 2 · SOUTHERN CALIFORNIA

Camper's Guide to CALIFORNIA

Parks, Lakes, Forests, and Beaches

Where to Go and How to Get There

ISBN 0-87201-153-4

Library of Congress Catalog Card Number 88-1686

10 9 8 7 6 5 4 3 2

This edition
was reviewed by the author and
reprinted March 1993.

Capital: Sacramento
Nickname: Golden State
Area: 159,000 square miles; ranks 3rd
Population: 26 million + (ranks 1st)
State Bird: California valley quail
State Flower: Golden poppy

State Tree: California redwood
Highest Elevation: 14,495 feet
  above sea level at Mt. Whitney
Lowest Elevation: 282 feet
  below sea level in Death Valley

Also of interest—

Birder's Guide to Northern California
Camper's Guide to British Columbia, Volumes 1 & 2
Camper's Guide to California Parks, Lakes, Forests, and Beaches/Volume 1—Northern California
Camper's Guide to Texas Parks, Lakes, and Forests/Third Edition
Hiking and Backpacking Trails of Texas, Third Edition
Camper's Guide to Florida Parks, Trails, Rivers and Beaches
Camper's Guide to Colorado Parks, Lakes, and Forests
Camper's Guide to Michigan Parks, Lakes, and Forests
Camper's Guide to Minnesota Parks, Lakes, and Forests
Skier's Guide to California, Volumes 1 & 2

CONTENTS

See Volume 1 for
Regions 1, 2, & 3

This Volume covers
Regions 4, 5, & 6

Region 4, page 1

Region 5, page 48

Region 6, page 97

Acknowledgments

The author is indebted to and wishes to thank the following agencies for information—in the form of maps, brochures, telephone conversations, and personal interviews—without which this book would not have been possible.

California Almanac,
California Department of Forestry
California Department of Parks & Recreation
California Office of Tourism
Mistix
National Park Service, Western Region
U.S. Bureau of Land Management
U.S. Army Corps of Engineers, Sacramento District
U.S. Forest Service, Pacific Southwest Region

Photo Credits

All photos are by the author unless credited otherwise:

California Department of Parks and Recreation, 21
California Department of Transportation, 35
California Office of Tourism, 8, 75, 78, 83, 138
Hearst San Simeon State Historical Monument/ California Department of Parks and Recreation, 41
Palm Springs Convention and Visitors Bureau, 106
Roaring Camp and Big Trees Railroad/California Office of Tourism, 13

Many places along California's beaches, such as this lighthouse near San Diego, offer good vantage points for whale watching (see page 138).

Introduction

California is truly a land of contrasts. The highest and lowest places in the contiguous United States are within sight of each other. Mt. Whitney rises to 14,495 feet while 85 miles away is Death Valley, whose lowest point is 282 feet below sea level. Extreme temperatures of −45°F and +135°F have been recorded, as have extreme yearly rainfall accumulations of zero in the desert and 161 inches in a rain forest.

From north to south, and east to west, California abounds with ideal recreation areas: forests of giant trees; high, rugged mountains; alpine meadows and lakes; fertile valleys; inland deserts; and, along the Pacific Ocean, rugged cliffs of the north coast and sandy beaches of the south coast. What better way is there to really see and enjoy the California outdoors than by camping?

The purpose of this *Camper's Guide* is to suggest places to go and provide directions to get there. You will discover information about the popular, well-known campgrounds as well as the lesser used camping areas. The public campgrounds presented in these two guides (see Volume 1 for Northern California) are provided and operated by federal and state agencies. Outdoor enthusiasts will find recreational opportunities at these sites that are as varied as one's imagination. You can swim, skin or scuba dive, sail, water ski, boat, canoe, raft, fish, picnic, backpack, bicycle, horseback ride, hike, walk along a nature trail, or kick up some dust with an off-road vehicle. In season, you can also cross-country ski, downhill ski, snow shoe, or snowmobile. You can pursue your favorite hobby as a bird watcher, photographer, botanist, geologist, or naturalist. You may choose to rough it at a primitive campsite or in the backcountry, or enjoy all of the comforts of home in a motor home. You can spend a day, a weekend, or an entire vacation doing what you like best, no matter how active, or inactive it is.

The number of public campgrounds in California's state and federal parks, lakes, and forests is staggering. Both volumes of this *Camper's Guide* contain recreational areas with camping facilities that comprise 106 state parks, covering more than 1 million acres of land; 4 state forests; 13 lakes administered by the U.S. Army Corps of Engineers; 14 na-

tional parks covering more than 4.6 million acres of land; and 44 campgrounds on some 17 million acres of Bureau of Land Management lands. There are also 19 national forests encompassing more than 20 million acres, with 4 million of these acres in 46 designated Wilderness Areas. You might be surprised to learn that the federal government controls about 45% of California's land: the U.S. Forest Service administers 20%; the Bureau of Land Management 17%; the Park Service 5%; and the Department of Defense 4%.

California's Seven Natural Wonders, as listed in the *California Almanac*, are Big Sur, Death Valley, Lake Tahoe, Mount Whitney, Pygmy Forest, Sutter Buttes, and Yosemite. The Sutter Buttes, perhaps not as well known as the others on the list, are near Yuba City and are known as the world's smallest mountain range.

The state is approximately 800 miles long and 300 + miles wide at its widest point, with an 840-mile coastline. California has less than 300 miles of gently sloping, sandy beaches, with pleasantly warm water, but of these, only half is publicly owned. Approximately 42% of the shoreline is not open to the public.

Enjoy your adventures in California, but don't fall into them! (You'll find sea caves and cavities all along the southern coast.)

California's Topography

In order to acquaint you with the general topography of California, let's take a quick trip around the state (see map above) to get an overall picture of the lay-of-the-land and what's available for recreational pursuits. Starting at the Mexico border on the Pacific Ocean, more than 200 miles of sun-washed sandy beaches stretch north to beyond Santa Barbara. These are the famed beaches enjoyed by swimmers and surfers almost year round. Offshore, the Channel Islands remain near wilderness and shelter a variety of marine life.

The Coast Range parallels the shore from just north of the Los Angeles Basin to the Oregon border. These mountains rise abruptly from the sea or from a narrow coastal plain. Around San Francisco they reach less than 4,000 feet, although some peaks in the north exceed 8,000 feet. For the most part, the north coast is a wild and rugged place where waves pound against the rocks, and groves of 300-foot tall redwoods grow.

East of the Coast Range is California's rich Central Valley, nearly 500 miles long and averaging 40 miles wide. Made up of the drainages of the Sacramento and San Joaquin Rivers, it is the largest agricultural region west of the Rockies, with some of the world's most productive acreage. The Sacramento/Stockton area has a huge maze of inland waterways. A Mississippi-style delta covers a thousand square miles and serves as the center for houseboating, a favorite sport in the area.

In the north, the Coast Range merges with the Cascade Range, forming a high, rugged area more than 200 miles wide. The Cascades rise to peaks and ridges 5,000 to 10,000 feet high. Massive and white, Mt. Shasta dominates the landscape, rising to a height of 14,161 feet. To the southeast, the Cascades merge with the Sierra Nevadas near Lake Almanor.

The Sierra Nevada, the largest mountain mass in the United States, is more than 400 miles long and 60 to 80 miles wide. Elevations increase from north to south as the range extends through Lake Tahoe, Yosemite, Kings Canyon, and Sequoia, then disappears into the Mojave Desert. In the north, few peaks exceed 8,000 feet while, south of Yosemite National Park the crest is 11,000.

To the west of the Sierras, gently rolling foothills covered with oaks and pine rise gradually from the Central Valley. The west slopes, cut by many rivers and streams, are generally moderate. Waterfalls plunge down the granite walls of Yosemite Valley, alpine lakes and backcountry trails lace the crest of the Sierra, where the deep-blue waters of Lake Tahoe straddle the California-Nevada border. The high country consists of many ridges, some parallel-

You might pan for the yellow metal in a park creekbed, like this one in the Sierra Nevada foothills, but the real gold is all around you.

ing the main crest, others branching away from it. The east slope of the Sierras drops steeply into Owens Valley.

East of Bakersfield, the Sierra Nevada meets the Tehachapi Mountains, which trend southwest, meeting the Coast Range and closing the south end of the Central Valley. Beyond, minor mountain ranges extend southeast to Mexico. The southeast quarter of California is a vast and fascinating area of three deserts—Mojave, Colorado, and Sonoran—extending to the Colorado River. Winter vacationers enjoy the warm winter days of the desert, which comes alive with a colorful spring wildflower bloom in February and March.

Your whirl-wind mini-tour of the state is now complete. The only thing that remains is to plan your next camping trip and pack your gear. You will, no doubt, agree that it may take a lifetime to see all that California has to offer. What a challenge! Go for it!

How to Use the Camper's Guide

The *Camper's Guide to California Parks, Lakes, Forests, and Beaches* comprises two separate volumes—Volume 1 covers Northern California and Volume 2 covers Southern California. (*Ed. note:* Yosemite National Park is in both volumes because of its popularity and pivotal position on the somewhat arbitrary north-south dividing line.) This second volume divides Southern California into the three geographic regions shown in the illustration. The parks, lakes, and forests within each region are arranged alphabetically and are cross-listed by name and city in the index. The first page of each region locates the park, lake, or forest on the map and gives the page number(s) where you can find more detailed information and maps of that specific area.

All the information in this *Camper's Guide* has been supplied by the respective operating agency, either through literature distributed by them, through verbal communication, or through secondary sources deemed reliable. The information presented is basic—it tells you how to get there, cites outstanding features of the area, and lists the facilities and the recreational activities available. Mailing addresses and telephone numbers are given in case you want additional information prior to your trip. For some parks, it's a good idea to confirm weather and road conditions before heading out.

The maps showing the location of facilities within a state or national park should be of considerable help. These maps are usually available to you at the park headquarters, but they can also aid you in planning a trip to an unfamiliar park. Those of you who have attempted to meet up with friends at a predetermined spot at a large campground can readily appreciate the value of having such a map. Most parks are easily found with the help of a good road map, but vicinity maps have been included here in some instances. Signs along the way can

also be relied upon after you reach the general vicinity of a park.

Because each ranger district within a national forest operates somewhat independently of the national forest as a whole, distributes its own materials, and in many ways has its own "personality" because of terrain, recreational opportunities, etc., information on each national forest is arranged by ranger districts. Visitors who wish to camp off-the-beaten-path should certainly purchase the official national forest map because even the best road map often does not show the many back roads in the forest.

The maps showing the location of the many recreation areas around a lake should also be of tremendous help to visitors. Perhaps this information will help to better distribute the visitors as they participate in various recreational activities that the lake has to offer. Several statistics about each lake have been included such as surface area in acres, the length of the lake, and the miles of shoreline. These facts can serve as a point of reference as you compare various lakes.

The facilities available at a campground often change, but a change in status usually means the addition of a service rather than a discontinuation. In other words, a camper often finds better and more facilities than those listed in the latest brochure.

May this *Camper's Guide* serve you well in the years ahead, whether you are a beginner or a seasoned camper. Take time to camp, to become *truly* acquainted with nature . . . and with yourself and your family! Don't put off until tomorrow what can be enjoyed today!

State Parks

Recreation! That's what California's State Park System means to millions of Californians and visitors. More than 250 state park units are located on over one million acres of land. Each park unit offers its own unique opportunities for fun and adventure, as illustrated by the range of titles—state park, . . . historic park, . . . beach, . . . reserve, . . . recreation area, . . . historical monument, . . . Wayside Campground, and . . . vehicular recreation area. Henceforth, they all will be referred to simply as "state parks." One hundred and six parks offer camping in one form or another, and so are included in this two-volume *Camper's Guide*. Volume 1 cites 50 state parks in Northern California and this volume cites 56 state parks in Southern California.

There are several types of campsites found in California state parks:

Developed campsites—ordinarily have improved roads, restrooms with hot showers, piped drinking water, and campsites with tables and stoves.

Primitive campsites—ordinarily have chemical or pit toilets in an informal area containing tables and central water supply, or in a designated area without facilities.

Trailer hookups—found at only a few parks; of course, trailers, campers, and motorhomes may also use developed or primitive campsites. Maximum lengths that can be accommodated must be considered by the park visitor.

Enroute campsites—day-use parking areas where self-contained trailers, campers, or motorhomes can be parked for one-night stays; they cannot be reserved in advance; enroute campers must leave by 9 a.m.

Environmental campsites—primitive sites that are isolated from each other and from the main campground; you must hike a short distance to reach them and sometimes carry in water and other supplies.

Selected information on camping that is basic to state parks in general is cited here rather than repeated for each park:

Some of the more popular parks fill up fast during peak months, so it's wise to be familiar with the campground reservation system on page I-6.

▲ Camping is allowed only in designated campsites.

▲ Family campsites will accommodate up to 8 persons and 2 licensed vehicles (including trailers); however, the campsite fee allows for the operation of only one motorized vehicle in the park. Additional motor vehicles, when permitted, will be subject to an "extra vehicle" fee of $3.00 per night.

▲ Campsites for groups are available at more than 50 state parks. Over 35 of them can be reserved through the State Park Reservation System (see page I-6). Some of them must be reserved directly with the park.

▲ Environmental campsites are available on a reservation basis through the Department of Parks and Recreation; maximum stay at any one campsite is 7 days and occupancy is limited to one family or 8 people. A fee is charged; pets are not allowed.

▲ Other types of campsites available at some state parks include individual trail camps, group trail camps, individual horse campsites, group horse camps, and hike and bike camps.

▲ Campsites for handicapped are available at many state parks and the facilities are handicapped accessible. Inquire.

▲ Length of stay at each campground is limited, with the range usually from 7 to 30 consecutive days, depending on the season. In addition, there is a limit of 30 days in any calendar year in that unit for general occupancy by the same persons, equipment, or vehicles.

▲ Camping fees vary for each classification of campsites: i.e., developed, hookups, developed with coastal access, primitive, enroute, and environmental.

▲ Reservations may be made at most parks through the State Park Reservation System (see page I-6) during the busy season. During "non-reservation" periods, campsites may be obtained on a first-come, first-served basis.

▲ Persons 62 years of age or older, verified by presentation of a valid driver's license or other identification card, will be allowed a discount of $2.00 at all state park campgrounds; and they will be allowed $1.00 discount at all state park units that charge for day-use on a per-vehicle basis.

▲ Visitors should remember that often a campground that is filled during the summer (or winter for desert parks) will have plenty of room at other times of the year, and even the busiest parks sometimes have vacancies during the week, from Sunday through Thursday nights.

▲ Dogs are allowed in state parks; a rabies certificate or license is required. During the day, it must be on a controlled leash no more than six feet long. Unless the dog is a seeing eye dog, it is not allowed in buildings or on trails nor on many beaches. At night, the dog should be in the tent or vehicle. There is a $1-per-night-per-dog fee in addition to the regular camping fee.

▲ Fires are permitted in park stoves and fireplaces, and gas-type cooking stoves may be used unless the area is posted otherwise. Down wood may not be collected for fuel.

▲ Flowers, rocks, plants, animals, artifacts, and other features of parks' natural and cultural history are protected by state law and may not be disturbed or collected. However, collection of driftwood is allowed, and rockhounding is permitted at some beaches.

▲ Horseback riding is restricted to trails designated for that purpose.

▲ For the off-highway-vehicle (OHV) enthusiast, there are five state vehicular recreation areas and two other state parks (Anza-Borrego Desert and Red Rock Canyon) that offer vehicular recreation opportunities on primitive dirt roads within their boundaries. OHV recreation is primarily financed through registration fees and gasoline taxes; use areas are provided for dune buggies, motorcycles, 4-wheel-drive, all-terrain vehicles, and snowmobiles. A very comprehensive and beneficial brochure entitled "Guide to Off-Highway-Vehicle Areas of California" is available from the Off-Highway Motor Vehicle Recreation Division of the California Department of Parks and Recreation. Phone number: (916) 322-7000

▲ A valid fishing license is required in order to fish in state park units.

▲ Hunting or the possession of loaded firearms is prohibited in all but a few units of the state park system.

▲ A folder entitled "Guide to California State Parks" is available for $2 from individual parks or from the Sacramento office. You can also request a free order form listing other departmental publications. For additional information about the California State Park System, contact:

    Department of Parks & Recreation
    P.O. Box 942896
    Sacramento, CA 94296-0001
    (916) 653-6995 (General Information)
    (916) 653-4000 (Publications)

Even if you bring your "home" with you, remember that the parks belong to everybody.

State Forests

There are 4 state forests in California, totaling some 67,000 acres, that allow camping. (three of them are covered in Volume 1—Northern California, and one, Mountain Home State Forest, with 7 campgrounds and 96 rustic campsites, is described on page 69 of this volume.) Foresters are involved in a very active program of timber harvest, enhancement of wildlife habitat, and protection of the watershed, along with consideration given to public recreation. Recreational activities available on state forest land include fishing and hunting in season in accordance with state laws and regulations, hiking, horseback riding, picnicking, and camping.

Facilities tend to be rustic; many campgrounds have pit toilets or no toilets, spring or creek water or no water. Although camping is free for the rustic facilities, a "campfire and special use permit" is usually required. These are obtainable from the individual forest headquarters. The camping season is normally May/June through November.

Kings Canyon National Park (page 62) can take your breath away, but what a way to go!

Reservation Systems

Campground reservations are necessary for popular parks in season, i.e., late spring, summer, and early fall. During the non-reservation periods family campsites are available on a first-come, first-served basis; this is the same basis for unreserved campsites during the reservation period. The list of parks/campgrounds requiring reservations and their reservation seasons changes from year to year. Even the agency handling the reservations can change so only basic information is given here. As a campground user, the best procedure is, each year, to obtain an up-to-date copy of each brochure describing the reservation procedure and containing the camping reservation application. The brochure also serves as a valuable source of information on facilities available. Reservations may be made up to 8 weeks in advance for family campsites and 12 weeks in advance for group campgrounds.

State Parks

For state parks, Ticketron was once used, then Mistix. To avoid confusion, the phrase "on State Park Reservation System" is used throughout this book to simply verify that the park/campground is usually on a reservation system. The reservation system is used extensively for state parks; three-fourths of the park units are presently using it—some year round and some seasonally. Thirty-eight of the park units use the reservation system for group campgrounds as well.

National Parks

Only 5 national parks in California are presently on a reservation system. Death Valley, Joshua Tree, Sequoia, and Whiskeytown each have one campground and Yosemite has 8 campgrounds on the Mistix reservation system.

National Forests

Selected national forest campgrounds in California are reservable through the Mistix reservation system. Presently, 13 national forests have reservable family campgrounds and 11 national forests have reservable group campgrounds. Because the reservable campgrounds may vary each year, obtain a current list from one of the forest supervisor's offices or from the Forest Service Public Affairs Office in San Francisco. Phone: (415) 705-2874.

For parks/campgrounds on the Mistix computerized reservation system, reservations may be made by phone, at an outlet or by mail. Phone orders may be charged to Visa or Mastercard. Informative brochures on the reservation system are updated yearly and are available for national parks as well as for California state parks. For information and reservations, phone the appropriate number listed below.

State parks in California
1-800-444-PARK (7275)

National parks
1-800-365-CAMP (2267)

National forests
1-800-283-CAMP (2267)

Los Padres National Forest is the only national forest in California that borders the Pacific Ocean.

National Parks

There are 20 national park service areas in California on 4.6 million acres. These areas include national parks, monuments, seashores, recreation areas, and historic sites. Fourteen of them provide camping facilities: 1 seashore; 2 recreation areas; 5 monuments and 6 parks. The word "park" is henceforth used as a general term to refer to all of the national areas. Seven national parks are located in the southern portion of California and are covered in this book (see map below).

Information on camping that is basic to national parks in general is cited here rather than repeated for each park:

▲ All parks have a visitor/information center containing interpretive displays and, sometimes, museums pertaining to that park. Most sell literature with in-depth explanations of history, geology, flora, and fauna. Usually an introductory film or slide show is offered.

▲ The visitor/information center should always be your first stop; brochures, maps, and a schedule of activities are readily available. Many of the large parks publish a newspaper outlining activities and other pertinent information about the park's services, features, and history.

▲ Both entrance fees and recreation use fees are authorized at many park areas. Entrance fees are not charged visitors under age 13 or over 61 (see page I-11 for "Federal Recreation Passport Program").

▲ Campsite users are charged recreation use fees at all campgrounds that have certain minimum facilities and services. They are charged in addition to any park entrance fee (see page I-11 for "Federal Recreation Passport Program").

▲ Fees for group campsites may vary with size of group, but most have a minimum charge of up to $10.

▲ Fees for concession-operated facilities are charged by the concessionaires and are not federal recreation use fees. They are not affected by either the Golden Eagle, Golden Access, or Golden Age Passports.

▲ Individual campsites are for use by an immediate family or a party of no more than 6 persons, including children.

▲ Most individual campsites are available on a first-come, first-served basis and cannot be reserved. An exception to this is that for the summer camping season, reservations can be made through Mistix for campsites at several parks. (see page I-6 for "Reservation Systems").

▲ Most parks require reservations for use of group campsites and hike-in campsites in the backcountry.

▲ The length of stay in most parks is 14 days; during the peak season at some parks, it may be 7 days; during the off-season it may be 30 days; at walk-in campsites it ranges from 1 to 3 days.

▲ Self-contained recreation vehicles—those requiring no utility connections—can be accommodated at most campgrounds, but size restrictions are imposed at some campgrounds.

▲ Sanitary (dumping) stations are available in some parks for disposal of liquid wastes from recreation vehicle holding tanks.

▲ Primitive camping is permitted in many of the remote, roadless areas of the park, but occasionally, backcountry use is prohibited because of emergency conditions—such as high fire danger or severe weather conditions. Check with the rangers at park headquarters to determine current conditions and to secure camping and/or fire permits, if needed.

▲ Backcountry use has been restricted in many areas and a quota system may be in effect. This program requires free permits for backcountry use, but limits the number of people permitted in the backcountry at one time. Contact the appropriate park for information about specific backcountry restrictions.

▲ Many parks have campgrounds that meet the needs of visitors in wheelchairs. Disabled visitors who have questions about their ability to use a particular campground should write to that park for more information.

▲ The gathering of wood for campfires is always limited to dead material found on the ground; sometimes it is prohibited. Campers are encouraged to use liquid-fuel campstoves or charcoal for cooking. Fires should be confined to fireplaces in established campgrounds and picnic areas.

▲ In many parks, interpretive programs, including nature walks, guided tours, and campfire talks are conducted by park personnel.

▲ Every area of a park is a museum of natural or human history; removal or destruction of any feature is not allowed. The ideal visitor "takes nothing but memories, leaves nothing but footprints."

▲ Do not feed wild animals. Food supplies should be locked up or hung out of reach; such measures are required at some parks.

▲ Hunting is prohibited in national parks and monuments. The use of campgrounds in these areas as base camps for hunting outside park boundaries also is prohibited. Hunting is authorized, in accordance with state laws, in national recreation areas and seashores.

▲ Fishing in all California parks requires a state fishing license.

▲ Pets are allowed in the parks and campgrounds if they are kept on a leash or under other physical restraint at all times. They are generally prohibited in backcountry areas.

▲ Areas classified as campgrounds have well-defined roads, parking spaces, and campsites. Drinking water and sanitary facilities, including flush toilets and refuse cans are furnished on a community basis. A typical campsite in a campground would include parking space, fireplace, table and bench combination, and tent space.

▲ In a walk-in campground or walk-in section of a campground, the parking space is provided but not as an integral part of each campsite.

▲ On the other hand, a camping area is an area (other than a campground) accessible by either road or trail where the facilities provided are minimal. Generally, they are limited to access roads, basic sanitary facilities, and a limited number of fireplaces and tables. Trail camps fall within this category.

▲ A group camp is an area designated for use by organized groups or other large parties. It is composed of one or more group spaces, each of which is provided with a large fireplace, several tables, and parking space for buses or a number of cars.

For further information, contact:

National Park Service
Western Regional Office
c/o Golden Gate National Recreation Area
Bldg 201, Fort Mason
San Francisco, CA 94123
(415) 556-0560

National Forests

California has 18 national forests within its boundaries, plus relatively small portions of Oregon's Rogue River and Siskiyou National Forests, and nearly 695,000 acres of Nevada's Toiyabe National Forest. The portions of the Toiyabe within California are included in this book since they have much to offer in the way of recreational facilities and activities. Shasta and Trinity National Forests, although two forests, were combined into one administrative unit in 1954 and are thus treated as one forest in this book. In addition, the Lake Tahoe Basin Management Unit is treated as a forest; it is an administrative unit established by the Forest Service in 1973 to manage all national forest lands in the Lake Tahoe Basin, rather than be managed by three different national forests that surround the area. Therefore, 19 national forests are included in this two-volume *Camper's Guide*. Volume 1 cites 12 national forests in Northern California, and this volume cites 7 national forests in Southern California (see map below).

The Forest Service of the U.S. Department of Agriculture is dedicated to the principles of multiple-use management of the nation's forest resources for sustained yields of water, forage, wildlife, wood, minerals, and . . . *recreation*. Yes, one of the main jobs of the Forest Service is to manage the national forests for recreation—all kinds, for all Americans. You can enjoy just about any kind of recreation on the 20 million acres of national forest land in California. The list of facilities/activities available include: equestrian facilities, pack stations, water skiing, marinas, boat rentals, swimming beaches, lake/reservoir fishing, stream fishing, hunting, wilderness areas, white-water rafting, ORV trails, snowmobiling, downhill ski areas, cross-country skiing, family and group campgrounds, dispersed camping, marked hiking trails, resorts with cabins, and picnic areas.

Selected information on camping that is basic to national forests in general is cited here rather than repeated for each forest:

▲ You must pay a fee to use certain developed sites and facilities. Such areas are clearly signed or posted as requiring a fee.

▲ Reservations are required for most group campgrounds through Mistix or the district ranger office, and a fee is charged.

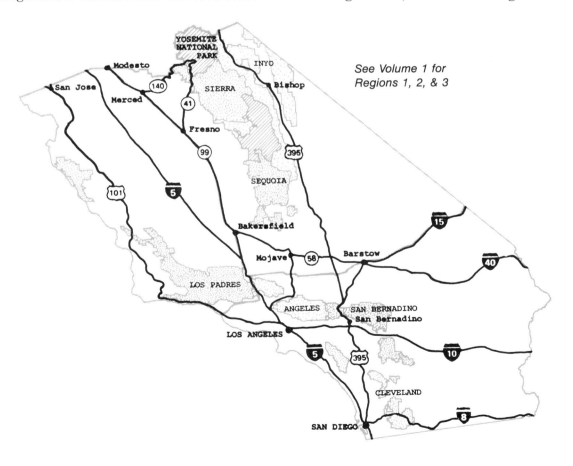

See Volume 1 for Regions 1, 2, & 3

▲ Where fees are required, you must pay them before using the site, facility, equipment, or service furnished.

▲ Individual family units are for use by one family or a party with a maximum of 6 people. Multiple family units are for use by 2 families or a party with a maximum of 12 people camping together.

▲ Most developed campgrounds have piped drinking water and provide toilet facilities of some type—either flush, vault, pit, or chemical.

▲ Undeveloped campgrounds have very few facilities and many do not have piped drinking water. The water supply is often from a spring, stream, river, or lake. It is recommended that water from such sources be treated by boiling it for 5 minutes.

▲ Golden Age and Golden Access Passports are honored.

▲ Most campsites are available on a first-come, first-served basis with no reservations accepted. Reservations for some family and group campgrounds can be obtained through Mistix (see page I-6 for "Reservation Systems").

▲ Limit of stay at most campsites is 14 days, but may be less in the more popular areas.

▲ In campgrounds, camp only in those places specifically marked or provided.

▲ Dispersed camping is allowed in most forests and is ideal for visitors with self-contained units, large groups, or for those who just want to get away from it all. Many areas are available, they have no facilities, are free of charge, but require a campfire permit, obtainable at the ranger district office.

▲ Obey restrictions on fires; they may be limited or prohibited at certain times. Within campgrounds and other recreation sites, build fires only in fire rings, stoves, grills, or fireplaces provided for that purpose.

▲ Barrier-free campgrounds and picnic grounds for physically handicapped visitors are available in most national forests. Inquire about facilities for handicapped visitors.

▲ The camping season differs from one forest to another and even within a forest. Campgrounds at higher elevations are usually open seasonally, being closed from late fall through spring because of snow conditions.

▲ Most campgrounds do not have garbage pickup so campers are expected to "pack out what you pack in."

▲ Pets must be restrained or on a leash while in developed recreation sites. Except for guide dogs, they are not allowed in swimming areas.

▲ Saddle or pack animals are allowed in recreation sites only where authorized by posted instructions.

▲ Within campgrounds and other recreation sites, use cars, motorbikes, motorcycles, or other motor vehicles only for entering or leaving, unless areas or trails are specifically marked for them.

▲ Obey area and trail restrictions on use of trail bikes and other off-the-road vehicles.

▲ Only travel on foot, horse, or pack animal is permitted in wilderness areas; motor vehicles and motorized equipment are not allowed.

▲ Both fishing and hunting are permitted in season in most forests, but a state license is required and state fish and game laws apply to national forest land.

▲ Indian sites, old cabins, and other structures, along with objects and artifacts associated with them, have historic or archeological value. Do not damage or remove any such historic or archeological resource.

▲ The forest has recently begun using a new "international symbol" sign to inform drivers which roads are not suitable for passenger cars, but are suitable for high clearance vehicles, such as pickups and 4-wheel drive trucks. The sign displays a passenger vehicle with a yellow, diagonal slash through it, highlighting the words "not recommended."

▲ Maps of each forest are available for $1.00 from the national forest offices and ranger stations. The maps show roads not on most road maps, so they are invaluable and necessary for visitors wishing to explore the backcountry.

▲ Visitors to a national forest are encouraged to visit either the office of the forest supervisor or the individual ranger district offices. They are able to supply you with numerous brochures on the various recreational activities, as well as give information on such items as road conditions, weather, campgrounds, dispersed camping areas, and fire conditions. For your convenience, addresses and phone numbers are included for each national forest.

The 18 California National Forests are administered by:
Forest Service
Pacific Southwest Region
630 Sansome Street
San Francisco, CA 94111
(415) 556-0122

Federal Recreation Passport Program

Some federal parks, refuges, and facilities can be entered and used free of charge. Other areas and facilities require payment of entrance fees, user fees, special recreation permit fees, or some combination. A 1987 brochure by the U.S. Department of the Interior entitled "Federal Recreation Passport Program" explains the five programs. Briefly stated, they are as follows:

Golden Eagle Passport

An annual entrance pass to those national parks, monuments, historic sites, recreation areas, and national wildlife refuges that charge entrance fees. It admits the permit holder and accompanying persons in a private, noncommercial vehicle. For those not traveling by private car, it admits the permit holder and family group. Cost, $25; good for one calendar year (January 1 through December 31); permits unlimited entries to all federal entrance fee areas.

Golden Age Passport

A free lifetime entrance pass for citizens or permanent residents of the United States who are 62 years or older. Also provides 50% discount on federal use fees charged for facilities and services except those provided by private concessionaires. Must be obtained in person, with proof of age.

Golden Access Passport

A free lifetime entrance pass for citizens or permanent residents of the U.S. who have been medically determined to be blind or permanently disabled and, as a result, are eligible to receive benefits under federal law. Offers same benefits as Golden Age Passport. Must be obtained in person, with proof of eligibility.

Locations where these three passes are obtainable include all National Park System areas where entrance fees are charged, all National Forest Service supervisor's offices, and most Forest Service ranger station offices.

Park Pass

An annual entrance permit to a specific park, monument, historic site, or recreation area in the National Park System that charges entrance fees. The park pass is valid for entrance fees only and does not cover use fees. Cost, $10 or $15, depending upon the area; good for one calendar year (January 1 through December 31); permits unlimited entries only to the park unit where it is purchased.

Federal Duck Stamp

Officially known as the Migratory Bird Hunting and Conservation Stamp and still required of waterfowl hunters, the federal Duck Stamp now also serves as an annual entrance fee permit to national wildlife refuges that charge entrance fees. The Duck Stamp is valid for entrance fees only and does not cover use fees. Cost, $10; good from July 1 through June 30 of the following year; permits unlimited entries to all national wildlife refuges that charge entrance fees. Can be purchased at most post offices.

Wilderness Areas

Nearly 4 million acres of the total 20 million acres of national forest land in California is now designated wilderness. Although many nonwilderness areas in the national forests provide similar opportunities for camping and hiking in an isolated, undeveloped setting, wilderness areas in particular are managed to preserve their natural conditions.

There is no wonder that wilderness areas in California's national forests attract more and more visitors every year as they offer something for everyone: rugged mountain slopes for experienced mountaineers; placid lakes for family campers; and a solitary getaway for people seeking isolation. Visitors are asked to observe no-trace camping practices in order to leave areas as undisturbed as possible.

Twenty-four wilderness areas are in the 7 national forests covered in this volume of the *Camper's Guide* (see map on next page). Be sure to get a map of the National Forest you intend to visit; they are available for $2.00 each. In addition, large topo maps (1 inch to the mile) are available for a few wilderness areas. An informative brochure entitled

Wilderness Areas of Southern California

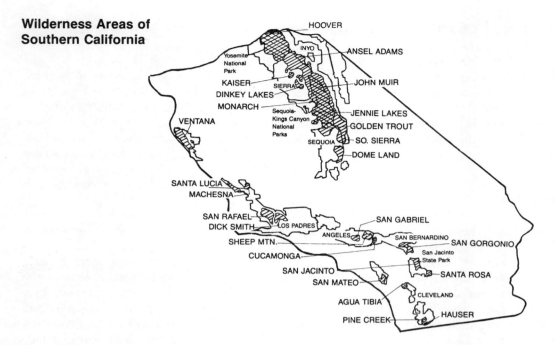

"Wilderness in the National Forests in California" will also prove helpful to those planning a trip to a wilderness area. All of these items are available from:

U.S. Forest Service
Office of Information
630 Sansome Street
San Francisco, CA 94111
(415) 556-0122

USGS topographic quad maps are available from many camping suppliers or in person from California offices of the U.S. Geological Survey in San Francisco, Menlo Park, and Los Angeles. You can obtain a free index map to select the quad map(s) you may need for your trip. Mail order sale of USGS quad maps is done only through their Denver office:

USGS Western Distribution Branch
Box 25286 Federal Center
Denver, CO 80225

As of 1985, a visitor permit is no longer required to enter some national forest wilderness areas. However, many areas do require permits, and some have a quota system for peak season use that admits visitors gradually in order to reduce adverse impacts on the wilderness quality of the areas. Group size is limited as very large groups have significantly greater impact on wilderness quality than small groups. Fishing and hunting are permitted in season in many wildernesses. If you don't want to camp in an area during hunting season, be sure to inquire about the effective dates when you plan your trip. Contact the forest supervisor's office of the national forest that you plan to visit for information about permit requirements and permit application forms.

A campfire permit is required if you plan to use a portable stove or build a campfire during your trip. During periods of severe fire danger, campfires may be prohibited and some areas or parts of areas closed to public entry. Be sure to inquire at the forest service office at your point of entry for complete information about any fire restrictions in effect.

Generally, a wilderness permit for entry into an area through a national forest is valid for travel through a contiguous area managed by the National Park Service and vice versa. Campfire permits are required in all areas. Specific restrictions regarding use of firewood, stock travel, and group size may vary from area to area.

For those who like to mix solitude with their splendor, California's wilderness areas are the perfect solution.

Lake Alpine on the Stanislaus National Forest is typical of the many lakes located on national forest lands. At such beautiful settings, there is something for all ages to enjoy.

U.S. Army Corps of Engineers' Lakes

Nearly all of the dams constructed in northern and central California by the U.S. Army Corps of Engineers were authorized to provide flood protection and irrigation water. These dams have created lakes, and in addition to accomplishing said objectives, they have created a wide variety of recreational opportunities. Recreation areas are administered by the Corps of Engineers at 13 such lakes/rivers; 6 of them are covered in this volume (Region 5).

Campgrounds are located at all 6 of the lakes/rivers; group campgrounds and boat-in camp sites are available at several of the areas. Camping is permitted only at designated sites/areas. There is a 14-day camping limit during any 30-consecutive-day period; Golden Age and Golden Access Passports are honored. Pets are not allowed on swimming beaches and should be penned, caged, physically restrained or on a leash less than 6 feet long in any developed recreation area.

Recreational activities include fishing, boating, swimming, waterskiing, snorkeling, scuba diving, hiking, and picnicking. Some of the lakes have horse trails. Refer to the facility chart for each lake for information regarding availability of piped water, hot showers, boat ramps, marinas and sanitary disposal stations. For further information, contact:

U.S. Army Corps of Engineers
Sacramento District
1325 J Street
Sacramento, CA 95814-2922
(916) 440-2183

U.S. Bureau of Land Management Camping Areas

The Bureau of Land Management (BLM), an agency of the Department of Interior, is responsible for the conservation, management, and development of 17.1 million acres of public land in California. The public lands are characteristic of the diversity that makes the Golden State unique. From the arid Southern California Desert, north to the Sierra Nevada Mountains, and west to the rugged North Coast, the public lands and resources administered by the BLM are some of the richest and most beautiful in the state.

Public lands offer a variety of recreational uses including camping, hiking, hunting, fishing, rock collecting, nature study, and off-road vehicle use. Most of the public lands offer numerous opportunities for camping near natural, scenic and historical resources. Some people prefer developed campsites, with amenities such as tent and recreational vehicle spaces, drinking water, boat ramps, picnic tables, or fireplaces. Others prefer "roughing it" in more primitive camping areas. The public lands have a wide variety of both types of campgrounds.

Reservations and Fees

Reservations generally are not required at BLM campgrounds except for group sites. All others are filled on a "first-come, first-served" basis. Overnight camping fees are charged at a number of these sites. The Golden Age Passport and the Golden Access Passport entitle the holder to use BLM recreation facilities for half the usual fee.

Water

If drinking water is not indicated on the chart, be prepared to carry your own or to purify existing water where available.

Hunting and Fishing

The public lands offer many opportunities for fishing and hunting, but state licenses are required. Contact the appropriate state agencies for information on seasons, creel, and bag limits.

Vehicle Use

Within campgrounds, vehicle use is allowed unless otherwise posted. Outside the campgrounds, established roads and trails provide the safest and least damaging travel routes. Some areas, because of fragile soils, critical wildlife habitat, or other reasons, have special ORV regulations.

Collecting

Rocks, minerals, and gemstones as well as berries, nuts, and flowers can usually be collected without a permit in reasonable quantities for personal use. A BLM permit is required for collection of large quantities or for commercial purposes.

Protecting Our Heritage

The public lands are rich in historical and archeological sites and related artifacts. Unfortunately, many of these irreplaceable links with the past are destroyed, either intentionally by vandals and thieves or unintentionally by casual collectors. These fragile resources are protected by federal law, and penalties for unauthorized collection include severe fines and imprisonment. Enjoy, but do not remove or disturb, these remnants of early American cultures.

For information in BLM camping areas contact:

U.S. Department of the Interior
Bureau of Land Management
California State Office
Sacramento, CA 95825
(916) 978-4754

Bakersfield District
Bureau of Land Management
800 Truxton Avenue, Room 302
Bakersfield, CA 93301
(805) 861-4191

California Desert District
Bureau of Land Management
6221 Box Spring Blvd.
Riverside, CA 92507
(714) 697-5200

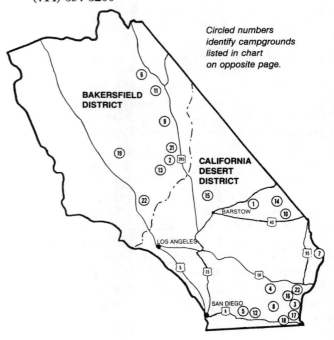

Circled numbers identify campgrounds listed in chart on opposite page.

BLM Camping Areas

Campground	Camping/Hiking	Trailers	Picnicking	Drinking Water	Hunting	Fishing	Swimming	Boating	Campsites	Location
1—Afton Canyon	X	X	X	X	X				22	40 mi. E. of Barstow on I-15, then 3 mi. S. on Afton Canyon Rd.
2—Chimney Creek	X	X	X	X	X				36	15 mi. W. of the junction of U.S. 395 and 9 Mile Canyon Rd.
3—Coon Hollow	X	X	X		X	X			27	27 mi. W. of Blythe via I-10. Take Wiley's Well Rd. exit, proceed 12 mi. to site.
4—Corn Springs	X	X	X	X	X				10	8 mi. E. of Desert Center via I-10, take Corn Springs exit, follow signs.
5—Cottonwood	X	X	X	X	X				25	2 mi. E. of Boulevard, California via county rd. to McCain Valley, then follow signs.
6—Crowley Lake	X	X	X	X	X	X		X	47	Via U.S. 395 to Crowley Lake Dr., 5½ mi. N. to Tom's Place.
7—Empire Landing	X	X	X	X	X	X	X	X		8 mi. NE of Earp on Parker Dam Rd. Site managed by Yuma, Arizona BLM Office.
8—Gecko*	X	X	X		X				120	From Brawley, 23 mi. E. on State Hwy. 78, 3 mi. S. on Gecko Rd.
9—Goodale Creek	X	X	X		X	X			62	12 mi. N. of Independence on U.S. 395 then 2 mi. W. on Aberdeen Cut-off Rd.
10—Hole-in-the-wall	X	X	X	X	X				22	From I-40, N. on Essex Rd. Right on Black Canyon Rd. for 10 mi. Follow signs to site.
11—Horton Creek	X	X	X		X	X			52	8½ mi. NW of Bishop via U.S. 395, 5 mi W. on Round Valley Rd.
12—Lark Canyon	X	X	X	X	X				20	2 mi. E. of Boulevard, California via county rd. to McCain Valley, then follow signs.
13—Long Valley	X	X	X	X	X				13	25 mi. W. of the junction of U.S. 395 and 9-Mile Canyon Rd. Follow signs on 9-Mile Canyon Rd. to site.
14—Mid Hills	X	X	X	X	X				26	I-40 to Essex Rd. Exit, N. on Essex Rd. to junction with Black Canyon Rd., then follow signs.
15—Owl Canyon	X	X	X	X					31	From I-15, 5 mi. N. of Barstow on Camp Irwin Rd. Then 5 mi. W. on Fossil Beds Rd.
16—Palo Verde Oxbow	X	X	X		X	X	X	X		3 mi. S. of Palo Verde, Calif. on CA Hwy. 78, turn E. onto gravel rd. Between mile posts 77 and 78. Follow gravel rd. 5 mi. to Colorado River. Site managed by Yuma, Arizona BLM office.
17—Senator Wash Reservoir	X	X	X			X	X	X		26 mi. NE of Yuma, Arizona via Imperial County Hwy S-24. Primitive facilities. Site managed by Yuma, Arizona BLM office.
18—Squaw Lake	X	X	X	X	X	X	X	X		20 mi. N. of Winterhaven on County Rd. S-24. Site managed by Yuma, Arizona BLM Office.
19—Squaw Leap	X	X	X		X	X	X		7	5 mi. NW. of Auberry on San Joaquin River off Hwy. 145.
21—Tuttle Creek	X	X	X		X	X			85	3½ mi. W. of Lone Pine, Calif. on Whitney Portal Rd., then 1½ mi. S. on Horseshoe Meadows Rd. Follow signs to site.
22—Walker Pass Trailhead	X	X	X	X					10	On State Hwy. 178 at Walker Pass (Access to Pacific Crest Trail).
23—Wiley Well	X	X	X		X				27	27 mi. W. of Blythe via. I-10, take Wiley's Well Rd. exit, proceed 9 mi. to site.

* No hiking.

Pacific Crest Trail

The Pacific Crest National Scenic Trail extends 2,560 miles from Canada to Mexico. In California the trail begins at the California-Oregon border south of Observation Peak in the Siskiyou Mountain Range, and ends at the Mexican Border near Campo. It passes through 14 national forests and 5 national parks in California, as well as several state parks and numerous wilderness areas (see page I-2).

The trail was established as part of the National System of Recreational and Scenic Trails by the National Trails System Act of 1968, and much of the route has been established only within the last 10 years. Although the trail extends along mountain ranges, there are stretches where there is no well-defined "Pacific Crest." Whatever your starting point and however long you plan to spend, the 1,615 miles of the trail in California offer challenge and beauty to match your pace and interest.

The Pacific Crest Trail crosses forests, brushland, mountains, and desert, and the weather and travel conditions differ as much from end to end as the vegetation and landscape. The stretch between Lake Tahoe and the Oregon border is snow-free until late in October. In the Sierra Nevada, snow comes early and stays late, so the best travel time is July through September. This segment of the trail is heavily used. In Southern California, winter and spring are generally the best times to travel.

The Trail is designed and intended for travel on foot or with stock. Travel by motorized vehicle is prohibited. You may travel with pets in national forests, national forest wildernesses, and on land administered by the Bureau of Land Management. However, pets are not allowed in national parks and state parks, so if your trip includes sections of either, you should leave your pet at home.

You will want to get detailed maps of the section of the Trail you plan to travel, either U.S. Forest maps or USGS quad maps. Many guidebooks, commercially available, have narrative descriptions of the trail and include trip maps. A brochure entitled "Pacific Crest Trail, the California Section" gives basic information you will need to plan your trip. It is available from the Office of Information of the U.S. Forest Service.

A permit is not required for travel on the Pacific Crest Trail as such, but a permit is required for travel through wilderness and other special areas, for overnight camping in southern California, and for use of portable campstoves or for building campfires in wildlands throughout the state. To make it simple, you can write the national forest (usually Cleveland National Forest, page 106) or national park office at your point of entry for a combined permit valid for one continuous trip on all parts of the Pacific Crest Trail in California. Please specify when and what segments of the trail you plan to travel. The Forest Service or national park personnel can then provide you with any special permits you will require or inform you of any special restrictions in effect.

I went to the woods because I wished to live deliberately, to front only the essential facts of life, and see if I could not learn what it had to teach, and not, when I came to die, discover that I had not lived.

—Henry David Thoreau

1—Andrew Molera State Park, 2
2—Atascadero (now Morro Strand)
   State Beach, 29
3—Big Basin Redwoods
   State Park, 3
4—Butano State Park, 4
5—Carpinteria State Beach, 45
6—Castle Rock State Park, 5
7—Channel Islands National
   Park, 6
8—Colonel Allensworth State
   Historic Park, 9
9—El Capitan State Beach, 44
10—Forest of Nisene Marks State
   Park, 10
11—Fremont Peak State Park, 11

12—Gaviota State Park, 43
13—George J. Hatfield State
   Recreation Area, 12
14—Henry Cowell Redwoods
   State Park, 13
15—Henry W. Coe State Park, 15
16—Hollister Hills State Vehicular
   Recreation Area, 17
17—Hungry Valley State Vehicular
   Recreation Area, 19
18—Julia Pfeiffer Burns
   State Park, 20
19—Los Padres National Forest, 22
20—Montana de Oro State Park, 30
21—Morro Bay State Park, 31
 2—Morro Strand State Beach, 29
22—New Brighton State Beach, 32
23—Pfeiffer Big Sur State Park, 33
24—Pinnacles National
   Monument, 34
25—Pismo Dunes State Vehicular
   Recreation Area, 36
26—Pismo State Beach, 37
27—Portola State Park, 38
28—Refugio State Beach, 42
29—San Luis Reservoir State
   Recreation Area, 39
30—San Simeon State Beach, 41
31—Seacliff State Beach, 46
32—Sunset State Beach, 47

MODESTO
Ceres
Atwater
MERCED
Madera
FRESNO
Tulare
Earlimart
McFarland
BAKERSFIELD
Santa Paula
Ventura
Gaviota
Lompoc
Guadalupe
SANTA MARIA
Arroyo Grande
SAN LUIS OBISPO
Morro Bay
Atascadero
Cambria
Coalinga
Soledad
MONTEREY
SALINAS
Castroville
Santa Cruz
Watsonville
Hollister
Tres Pinos
Los Banos
Santa Clara
SAN JOSE

Channel Islands National Park

Andrew Molera State Park

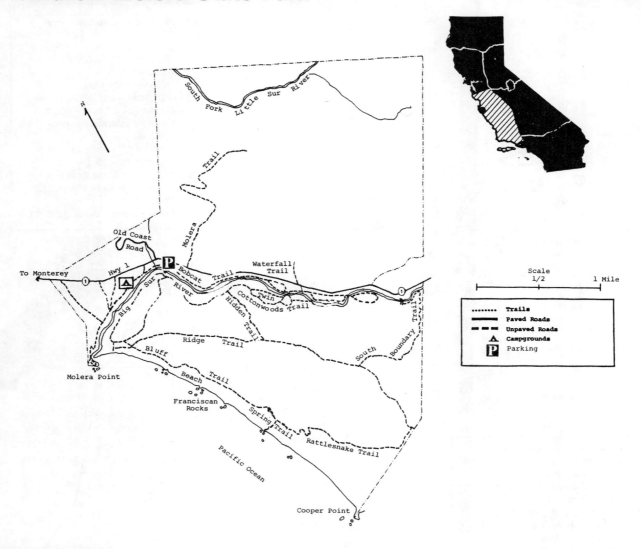

For Information

Andrew Molera State Park
% Pfeiffer Big Sur State Park
Big Sur, CA 93920
(408) 667-2315

Facilities & Activities

primitive walk-in campsites
no showers
fishing
hiking trails
swimming
horseback riding trails

Location

Andrew Molera State Park is located 21 miles south of Carmel on Highway 1. This 4,786-acre park, at an elevation of 60 feet, is in Monterey County.

Special Notes

The trail camp is a 5 minute walk from the parking lot. There are more than 16 miles of trails. One can hike or travel by horseback on these trails along bluffs overlooking 3 miles of beach, climb Molera Ridge through a chaparral environment, or follow the Big Sur River Valley through oak woodlands, redwoods, and stands of sycamores and maples. This park has the rugged scenic beauty typical of the Big Sur Coast.

Big Basin Redwoods State Park

For Information

Big Basin Redwoods State Park
Big Basin, CA 95006
(408) 338-6132

Location

Big Basin Redwoods State Park is located 20 miles north of Santa Cruz via SH 9 and SH 236. This 15,647-acre park, at an elevation of 1,000 feet, is in Santa Cruz and San Mateo counties.

Facilities & Activities

4 campgrounds
143 developed campsites
45 developed walk-in sites
campsites for disabled at Blooms Creek
showers
27-foot trailers; 30-foot campers/motorhomes
trailer sanitation station at Huckleberry
    Campground
6 trail camps for backpackers
2 group camps—on State Park Reservation
    System (Sequoia, all year; Sky Meadow,
    May—Oct.)
    Sequoia (3 sites, each with 50 person/12 vehicle
        max.; showers)
Sky Meadow (2 sites, each with 50 person/12
    vehicle max.; no showers)
picnicking
hiking trails (approx. 100 miles)
nature trails
museum/nature center
horseback riding trails
food service
supplies
on State Park Reservation System (all year)

Special Notes

Acquired in 1902, this is the oldest park in the California State Park System. It has 4 beautiful waterfalls, the highest of which is 65-foot Berry Falls, a wide variety of environments, plenty of animals, and lots of bird life. However, the stately redwood groves are the big attraction in the park.

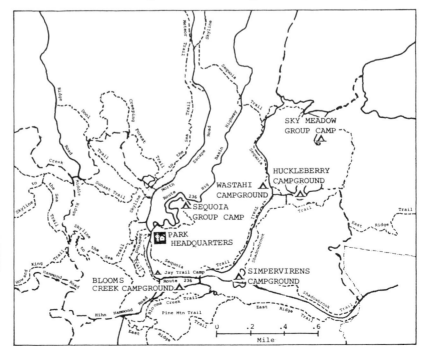

Legend:
.... Trails
———— Paved Roads
— — — Unpaved Roads
▲ Campgrounds

Butano State Park

For Information

Butano State Park
P.O. Box 9
Pescadero, CA 94060
(415) 879-0173

Location

Butano State Park is located midway between Santa Cruz and Half Moon Bay, 5 miles south of the community of Pescadero and 3 miles east of coastal Highway 1 on Cloverdale Road. The 2,186-acre park is at 500 feet elevation in the Santa Cruz Mountains of southern San Mateo County.

Facilities & Activities

21 developed campsites
19 developed walk-in sites
no showers
24-foot trailers; 27-foot campers/motorhomes
Butano Trail Camp for backpackers
picnicking
hiking trails
on State Park Reservation System (drive-in, all
    year; walk-in, April—Sept.)

Special Notes

Campers at Butano State Park enjoy a bit of secluded wilderness. Use of the Butano Trail Camp must be arranged in advance. Ground fires are not allowed because of fire danger. Dogs are not permitted on the trails.

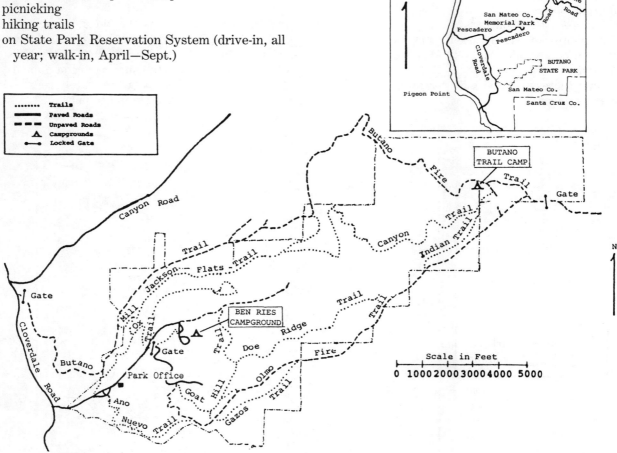

Castle Rock State Park

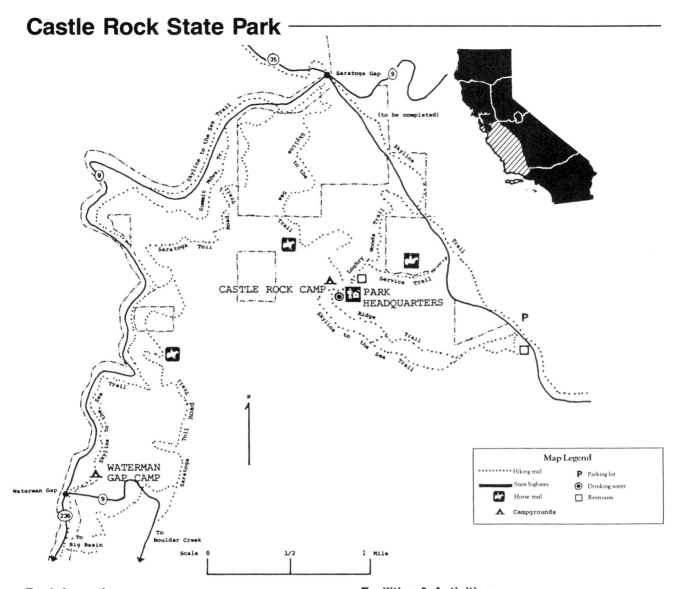

Map Legend

.... Hiking trail

▬▬▬ State highway

🐴 Horse trail.

⛺ Campgrounds

P Parking lot

◉ Drinking water

☐ Restroom

For Information

Castle Rock State Park
15000 Skyline Blvd.
Los Gatos, CA 95030
(408) 867-2952

Facilities & Activities

25 primitive walk-in campsites
picnicking
hiking trails (23 miles)
nature trails
horseback riding trails

Location

Castle Rock State Park perches on the western ridge of the Santa Cruz Mountains, which separate San Francisco Bay from Monterey Bay. The main entrance to the park is the parking lot off of SH 35, 2.5 miles southeast of Saratoga Gap (the intersection of SH 9 and SH 35). The 3,024-acre park is in Santa Cruz County and reaches 3,215 feet in elevation.

Special Notes

Castle Rock can only be experienced via the trails that travel through many different plant and animal communities, and pass by rock outcroppings, vista points, a waterfall, and park headquarters. The "Skyline to the Sea Trail" is 34 miles to the ocean through Big Basin Redwoods State Park. The rocks, especially Castle Rock and Goat Rock, offer excellent opportunities for rock climbing.

Channel Islands National Park

For Information

Superintendent
Channel Islands National Park
1901 Spinnaker Drive
Ventura, CA 93001
(805) 644-8262

Location

Channel Islands National Park consists of five islands off of southern California's mainland coast—Anacapa, San Miguel, Santa Barbara, Santa Cruz, and Santa Rosa, although the latter two are still privately owned. The closest island to the mainland, Anacapa, lies 11 miles southwest of Oxnard and 14 miles from Ventura. Access to the islands is by boat only. The visitor center and park headquarters are reached by taking the Victoria Avenue exit off of U.S. 101 at Ventura, if northbound, and the Seaward Avenue exit off of U.S. 101, if southbound. Follow Channel Islands signs on Harbor Boulevard south to Spinnaker Drive. The park concessioner boat service, Island Packers, is also located on Spinnaker Drive.

Special Notes

The islands are rookeries for gulls, cormorants, brown pelicans and other seabirds. Sea lions and harbor seals are often seen. In December through March, the annual gray whale migration passes close to Anacapa Island. The waters for 1 nautical mile around Anacapa, San Miguel, and Santa Barbara Islands are California State Ecological Reserves. State fish and game regulations apply. Fishing requires a California fishing license. Marine life in Anacapa landing cove area is totally protected.

On Anacapa, Santa Barbara, and San Miguel Islands, all plants, animals, rocks, and other natural archeological and historic features are protected and may not be disturbed, destroyed or taken. There are accessible tidepools on Santa Barbara, San Miguel, and West Anacapa. Do not collect anything; collecting is illegal.

The authorized park concessioner boat service is:

Island Packers
1867 Spinnaker Drive
Ventura, CA 93001
Reservations: (805) 642-1393
Information: (805) 642-7688

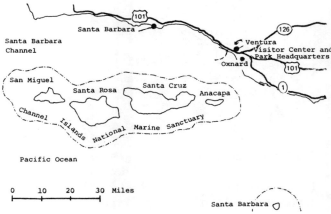

Weather permitting, boats run regularly throughout the year to Anacapa but less often to Santa Barbara, mainly from Memorial Day to Labor Day. Reservations are recommended.

If you plan to take your own boat to the islands, refer to National Ocean Survey Charts 18720, 18729, and 18756. To go ashore on Anacapa or Santa Barbara Islands requires a skiff, raft or small boat.

Anacapa Island is almost 5 miles long with a total land area of about 1 square mile. Anacapa is composed of 3 small inlets inaccessible from each other except by boat. To protect the pelican rookery, West Anacapa is closed to the public except at Frenchy's

Anacapa Island

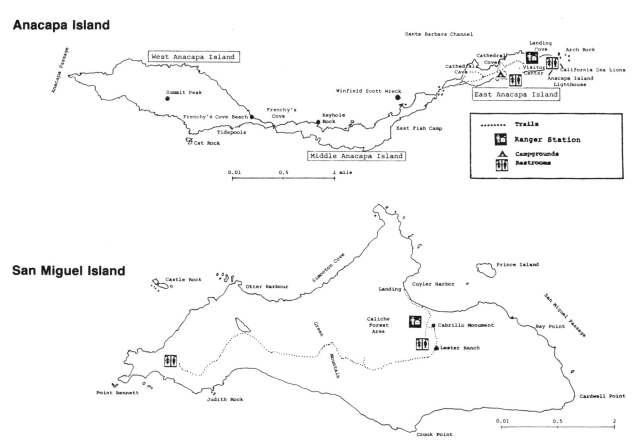

San Miguel Island

Cove. There is a beach and fine snorkeling area at Frenchy's Cove on West Anacapa and the area on the south side is noted for its tidepools. Most visitors go to East Anacapa Island. Picnicking is allowed; there are latrines but no fresh water. A self-guiding nature trail is located near the small ranger station. Do not visit the lighthouse when the fog horn is on as severe hearing damage may result. Beaches on East Anacapa are not accessible, but on calm summer days you may swim in the landing cove. Camping is restricted to the campground on East Anacapa. There are no shade trees on the island and no telephone. Guided walks and evening programs are available.

Santa Cruz Island, the largest and most diverse of the islands is about 24 miles long, with a 77-mile coastline and a land area of about 96 square miles. Devil's Peak, the highest of all the mountains on the Channel Islands stands at 2,400 feet. The island is privately owned and you must have a permit to land. The Nature Conservancy conducts day-trips to the island for educational groups and once each month for the general public in May through November. Camping is not permitted.

Santa Rosa Island, the second largest park island, is 15 miles long, 10 miles wide, and has 53,000 acres of remarkable contrasts: cliffs, high mountains, deeply cut canyons, gentle rolling hills and flat marine terraces. Vast grasslands blanket about 85% of the island. Santa Rosa Island is privately owned and landing on it requires advance permission of the owners. Camping is not permitted.

San Miguel Island, the westernmost of the islands, is 8 miles long and 4 miles wide. It is primarily a plateau of 400–500 feet in elevation with two rounded hills that emerge from its windswept landscape. A permit to land on San Miguel must be obtained in advance of your visit from park headquarters. The island is open for seasonal day use only and all visitors who wish to hike beyond the beach at the harbor must be accompanied by a park ranger. The island is managed cooperatively between the U.S. Navy, which administers the island, and the National Park Service, which manages it. Camping is not permitted.

Santa Barbara Island, south of the other 4 park islands, is small and triangular. The 640-acre island has steep cliffs that rise to a marine terrace topped

Santa Barbara Island

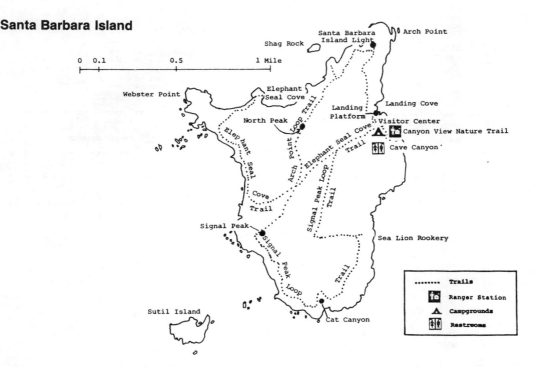

by two peaks. The highest point, Signal Peak, is 635 feet in elevation. Camping is allowed only in the campground. The island offers 5½ miles of trails to explore as well as a self-guiding nature trail near the ranger station. There is no telephone. Latrines are provided. Visitors must bring their water.

Facilities & Activities

* primitive camping only at Anapaca Island and Santa Barbara Island
camping restricted to a designated area
access by boat only
no fee; reservations required; 14-day limit
30-person limit at each island
pit toilets; table; fire grills
small mountain tents recommended because of the wind
no drinking water; fuel, supplies, etc.
no open fires in grills from May to October and during other dry periods
(* Note: campers should pack their belongings and food in backpacks, duffle bags, and containers with handles as everything goes ashore in a skiff, is passed up a ladder and later carried up a hill to the campground. At Santa Barbara it is less than ¼ mile but at Anacapa the distance is more than ½ mile.)
day use on San Miguel by permit only

concessioner boat service from mainland to the islands
self-guiding nature trails
hiking on established trails only
picnicking
snorkeling
SCUBA diving
swimming, though no accessible sand beach on either island
boating
fishing (landing cove at Santa Barbara only)
regularly scheduled evening programs/ exhibits/movies at headquarters visitor center

You'll definitely give Channel Islands National Park a "seal of approval" when you see its abundant wildlife.

Colonel Allensworth State Historic Park

For Information

Colonel Allensworth State Historic Park
Star Route 1, Box 148
Earlimart, CA 93219
(805) 849-3433

Location

Colonel Allensworth State Historic Park is located 20 miles north of Wasco on Highway 43, 15 miles west of Earlimart on County Road J22. In Tulare County, at 205 feet elevation, the park encompasses 240 acres.

Special Notes

The park is at the site of the only California town to be founded, financed, and governed by black Americans. Incorporated in 1908, the new town grew rapidly at first but began to lose population during the 1920s and 1930s. Small groups can arrange to use the dormitory.

Facilities & Activities

15 developed campsites
2 campsites for disabled
no showers
30-foot trailers; 30-foot campers/motorhomes
picnicking
exhibits
visitor center open daily
group tours by reservation
on State Park Reservation System (April—Nov.)

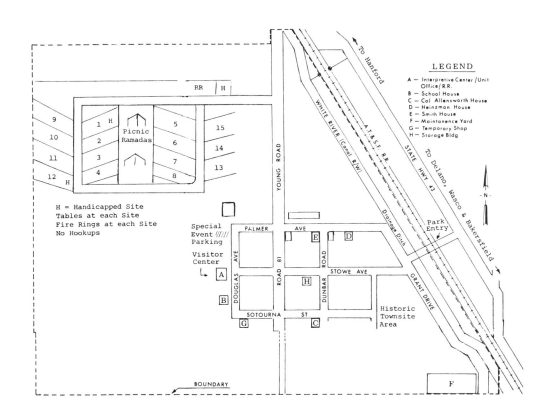

Forest of Nisene Marks State Park

Facilities & Activities

hike-in trail camp (reserve with park)
picnicking
hiking trails

Special Notes

To stay overnight at the Westridge Trail Camp you must make advance reservations. Only backpacking stoves are allowed year-round at the trail camp. There is drinking water and a restroom at the facility. Fifteen miles of trails lead from cool redwood forests to the warmer upper ridges. Many of the hiking trails that had been placed atop hundred-year-old railroad grades were washed away during the winter storms of 1982 and 1983. Some trails have been restored on the Bridge Creek and West Ridge sides of the park, but it may be many years before the hiking trail system is once again extended into the farthest reaches of the Aptos Creek Canyon. The park has more than 30 miles of hiking trails and fire roads for public use.

The Forest of Nisene Marks State Park is on land that was clear-cut of redwood trees during a 40-year logging frenzy (1883–1923). When the loggers left the Aptos Canyon, the forest began to heal itself and now the scars grow fainter with each passing year. The forest's land is a maze of ridges and canyons formed by the twisting and contorting of the earth due to faults that run diagonally across the park.

For Information

Forest of Nisene Marks State Park
101 North Big Trees Park Road
Felton, CA 95018
(408) 335-9145

Location

The Forest of Nisene Marks State Park is located 4 miles north of Aptos on Aptos Creek Road. In Santa Cruz County, this park offers 9,960 acres of rugged semi-wilderness rising from sea level to steep coastal mountains of more than 2,600 feet.

Fremont Peak State Park

For Information

Fremont Peak State Park
P.O. Box 1110
San Juan Bautista, CA 95045
(408) 623-4255

Location

This state park is located in Monterey and San Benito counties 11 miles south of San Juan Bautista on San Juan Canyon Road. The 244-acre park has an elevation of 2,750 feet.

Facilities & Activities

25 primitive campsites
18-foot trailers; 26-foot campers/motorhomes
6 group camps (each with 50 person max.)
picnicking
group picnicking area (40 max.)
hiking trails (4 miles)
nature trails

Special Notes

The road to the park winds up through canyons and over ridges studded with oak, pine, and madrone to an elevation of 3,000 feet above the village of San Juan Bautista. Grasslands in the higher peaks of the Gavilan Range feature plenty of hiking trails with expansive views of Monterey Bay. The clear air makes this park a favorite spot for amateur astronomers.

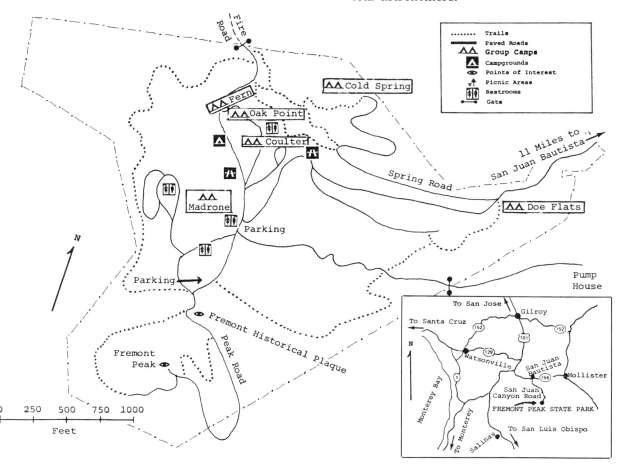

George J. Hatfield State Recreation Area

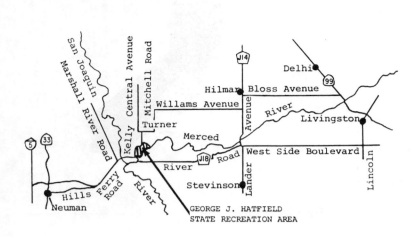

For Information

George J. Hatfield State Recreation Area
4394 Kelly Road
Hilmar, CA 95324
(209) 632-1852

Location

George J. Hatfield State Recreation Area, a 47-acre park, is located approximately 10 miles east of I-5 at the Newman exit; head east on J18 to Kelly Road. At a 62-foot elevation, the park is situated in the midst of San Joaquin Valley farmlands on the banks of the Merced River in Merced County.

Facilities & Activities

21 developed campsites for tents
no showers
RVs park in parking lot (21-foot max.)
group camping area (200 person/40 vehicle max.)
picnicking
group picnicking area (350 max.)
fishing
hiking trail
swimming

Special Notes

The recreation area is bordered on three sides by the Merced River, giving it 1¼ miles of river frontage. There are several sandy beaches for play. The camp and picnic areas are dotted with valley oak, box elder, cottonwood, maple, and Modesto ash.

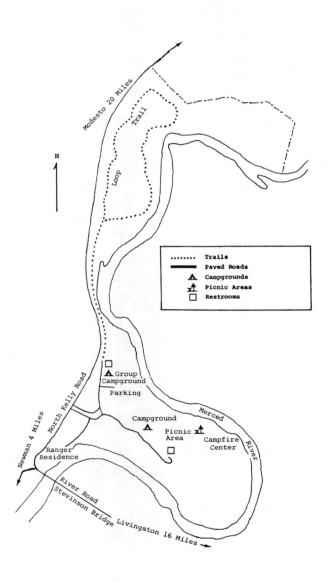

Henry Cowell Redwoods State Park

Road. The park is in Santa Cruz County and has 4,082 acres and an elevation of 500 feet.

For Information

Henry Cowell Redwoods State Park
101 North Big Trees Park Road
Felton, CA 95018
(408) 335-4598

Location

Henry Cowell Redwoods State Park is located 5 miles north of Santa Cruz on Highway 9. The campground is 3 miles east of Felton on Graham Hill

Facilities & Activities

113 developed campsites
campsites for disabled
showers
27-foot trailers; 35-foot campers/motorhomes
trailer sanitation station
picnicking
group picnicking area (200 max.)
fishing
hiking trails (15 miles)
swimming (San Lorenzo River)
nature trails
exhibits
horseback riding trail (15 miles)
food service
on State Park Reservation System (April—Oct.)

Thanks to Henry Cowell, Sr. and Joseph Welch, who in the 1880s decided to protect a virgin forest of coastal redwoods, this train carries people through the forest instead of carrying trees out of it.

Henry Cowell Redwoods State Park   13

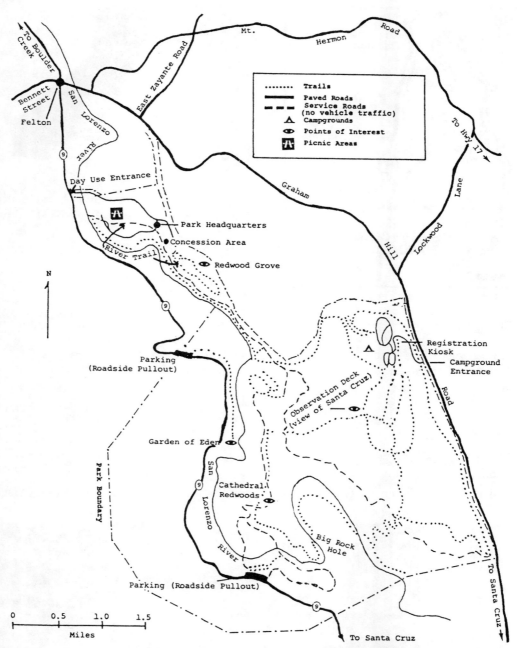

Special Notes

This is the home of the Redwood Grove, with its self-guided nature path. The park has a coast redwood tree 285 feet in height. You can also find Douglas fir, madrone, oak and the most unusual feature of the park, a stand of Ponderosa pine.

When the winter runs of steelhead and silver salmon begin, many anglers visit the park to test their skill and tackle on these lively game fish. Fishing season is from mid-November to the end of February; the river is closed to fishing the rest of the year.

The semi-wilderness area lying south and west of the campground can be reached by one of the three hiking and riding trails that pass through the campground. The Rincon Trail, which intersects with the Ridge Trail midway through the park, originates from a parking lot alongside Highway 9 at the park's south end. It passes by the Cathedral Redwoods, a ring of trees growing from a single base.

Henry W. Coe State Park

For Information

Henry W. Coe State Park
P.O. Box 846
Morgan Hill, CA 95038
(408) 779-2728

Location

Henry W. Coe State Park, essentially a wilderness park, has 32,230 acres of solitude. Located 14 miles east of Morgan Hill on East Dunne Avenue, it is in Santa Clara and Stanislaus counties. The campground has an elevation of 2,200 feet, with elevation ranges from 1,200 to 3,100 within the park.

Facilities & Activities

20 primitive campsites
no showers
18-foot trailers, 26-foot campers/motorhomes
21 campsites for backpackers (permit required)
hike-in group camp at Manzanita Point (10 sites, each with 50 person/1 vehicle max.; bring own water; primitive)—reserve through park
fishing
hiking and riding trails (40 miles)

Pine Ridge Museum
equestrian camping at 3 sites—reserve through park
Headquarters (8 horses/riders, corrals, water available, trailer in)
Manzanita Point (30 horses/riders, hitching rails, pond)
Shaffer's Corral (20 horses/riders, corrals, creek)

Special Notes

The park is an undeveloped expanse and is therefore most enjoyable to those who are willing to do without the conveniences of modern life to experience more vividly the wonders and the challenges of nature. Spring and fall are the most popular times to visit the park. During the summer, midday

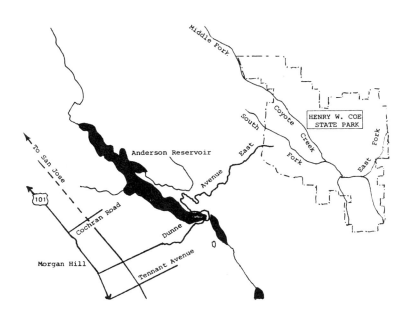

temperatures are likely to range in the nineties or higher; in the winter, frost and occasional light snow occur at the higher elevations. Rainstorms are common between November and March.

Extreme dryness during the long summer season can result in almost explosive fire conditions throughout the Hamilton Range. During the fire season all fires, including stoves, may be prohibited, or the back country may be closed to over-night use. Though water is available at many springs and creeks throughout the park during the year, these sources may be limited or disappear during the hot summer months, so water must then be packed in from park headquarters. All back country water should be purified before use.

Pine Ridge Museum, open from 9–4 on Saturdays and Sundays only, interprets ranch life in the late 1880s.

Hollister Hills State Vehicular Recreation Area

For Information

Hollister Hills State Vehicular Recreation Area
7800 Cienega Road
Hollister, CA 95023
(408) 637-8186

Location

Hollister Hills State Vehicular Recreation Area, located in San Benito County in the Gabilan Mountains, is 8 miles south of Hollister via Cienega Road. The 3,322-acre park's elevation ranges from 660 feet to 2,425 feet.

Facilities & Activities

3 family campgrounds at the Lower Ranch
100 primitive campsites
showers at Lodge Camp
2 group camps at the Upper Ranch—reserve
  through park
  Sycamore (60 persons)
  Garner Lake (200 persons, showers)
picnicking
hiking trails
nature trails
food service on weekends
trails and open area for off-road vehicle use

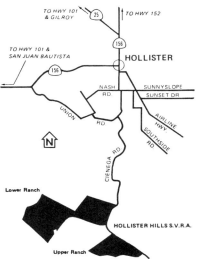

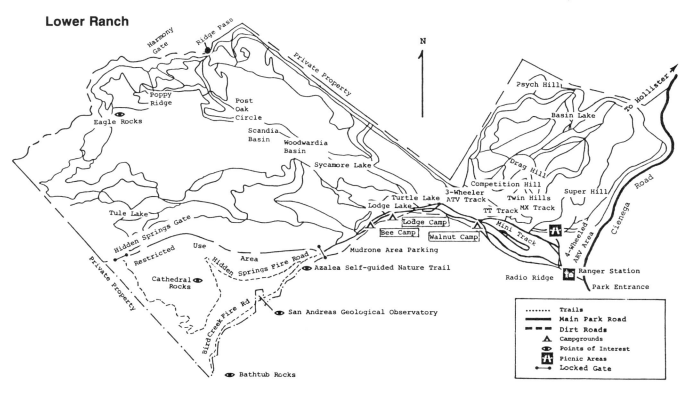

Lower Ranch

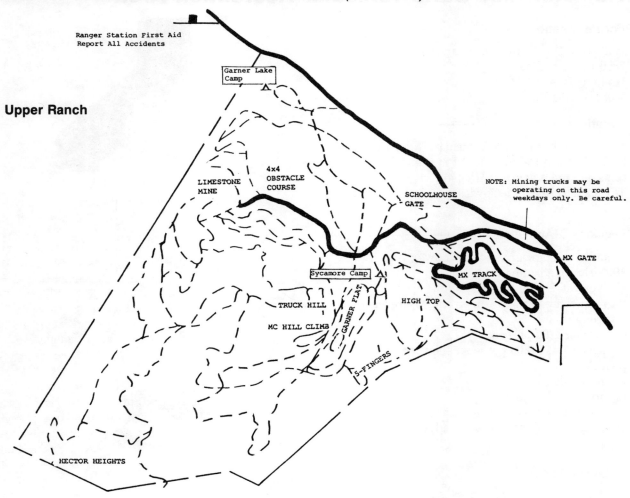

Ranger Station First Aid
Report All Accidents

Garner Lake Camp

Upper Ranch

4x4 OBSTACLE COURSE

LIMESTONE MINE

SCHOOLHOUSE GATE

NOTE: Mining trucks may be operating on this road weekdays only. Be careful.

MX GATE

Sycamore Camp

MX TRACK

TRUCK HILL

GARNER FLAT

HIGH TOP

MC HILL CLIMB

5-FINGERS

HECTOR HEIGHTS

Special Notes

Hollister Hills SVRA offers recreation for motorcyclists, 4-wheelers, picnickers, and campers. The park straddles the San Andreas Fault, and you can see the rift along Bird Creek; the east side is above soil and the west side is granite. The ranch was opened to public riding in 1970 and became a state vehicular recreation area in 1975.

With two ranches, this is an off-road vehicle paradise. The Upper Ranch, an 800-acre area that has about 60 miles of trails, is used for 4-wheel-drive recreation and for 4-wheel-drive and motorcycle special events; a fenced motocross track is also located here. Four-wheel-drive operators should call before coming, especially on weekends, to make sure that the area isn't reserved for a special event. To use the area for the day, register first at the park

office. A 4-wheel-drive obstacle course was built in 1982 and is located on Foothill Road. Four-wheel drive and motorcycle clubs can reserve the Upper Ranch for special events.

The 2,400-acre Lower Ranch, set aside for motorcycle and ATV use only, has about 80 miles of trails and several hillclimbs. There is also a TT track, a mini-bike trail, and a mini-track. Riding is permitted from sunrise to sunset. A special area has been set aside for use only by larger 4-wheeled ATVs such as Odysseys. For safety reasons, these vehicles are not allowed on roads or trails designated for motorcycle use.

A small area in the southwest corner of the Lower Ranch is closed to vehicle use. In this area you can hike the Azalea Canyon self-guided nature trail and several miles of hiking trails, enjoying cool canyons where it's damp enough for ferns and azaleas to grow.

Hungry Valley State Vehicular Recreation Area

For Information

Hungry Valley State Vehicular Recreation Area
Box 1360
Lebec, CA 93243
(805) 248-6447

Location

Set in the rolling hills of northern Los Angeles and Ventura counties, the 19,000-acre Hungry Valley State Vehicular Recreation Area's entrance is at a U.S. Forest Service Campground, 1 mile north on Peace Valley Road from I-5. Hungry Valley is at 4,000 feet elevation.

Facilities & Activities

primitive camping in a 1,600-acre area in Hungry Valley
chemical toilets
no water
primitive camping also permitted in Quail Canyon area in connection with special events there
trails and open area for unrestricted off-road vehicle use
hiking into the natural preserve

Special Notes

This area offers a variety of terrains for motorcycle, 4-wheel-drive and dune buggy enthusiasts—more than 15,000 acres available for trail riding. Spring and fall offer Hungry Valley's best weather. Summer days are hot, dry, and often windy. In winter, occasional snow blankets the surrounding hills. The hot, dry windy summers bring extreme fire danger, and there is the possibility of wildfires at other times of year. Ground fires, barbecues, and hibachis are prohibited.

The 1,500-acre Quail Canyon area, accessible from Peace Valley Road, can be reserved for motorcycle and 4WD club and competitive events. For a change of pace, you can hike into the natural preserve, where a seep provides water for valley oak and native grasses.

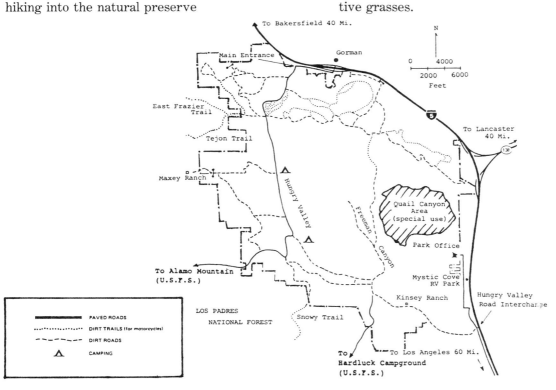

Julia Pfeiffer Burns State Park

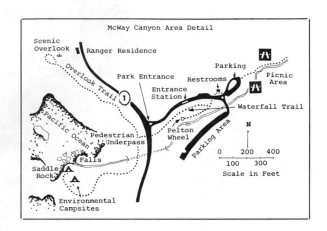

McWay Canyon Area Detail

Scenic Overlook
Ranger Residence
Overlook Trail
Park Entrance
Parking
Restrooms
Picnic Area
Entrance Station
Waterfall Trail
Pelton Wheel
Pacific Ocean
Pedestrian Underpass
Parking Area
Falls
Saddle Rock
Environmental Campsites

N

0   200   400
  100   300
Scale in Feet

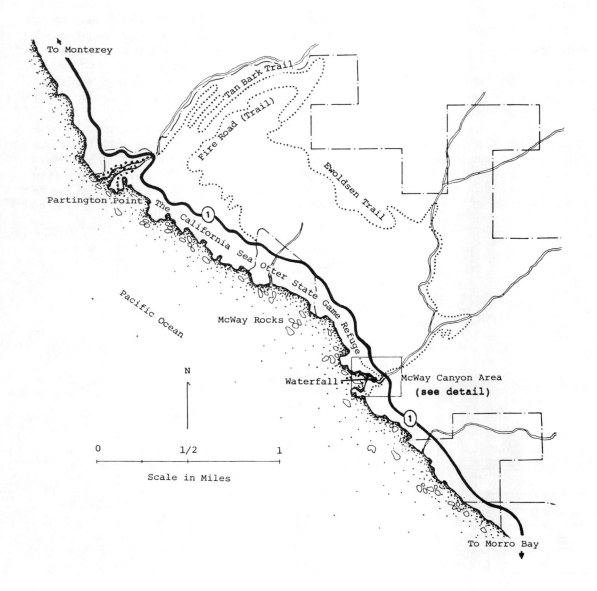

To Monterey

Tan Bark Trail

Fire Road (Trail)

Ewoldsen Trail

Partington Point

Pacific Ocean

The California Sea Otter State Game Refuge

McWay Rocks

Waterfall

McWay Canyon Area
(see detail)

N

0   1/2   1
Scale in Miles

To Morro Bay

Julia Pfeiffer Burns State Park *(continued)*

For Information

Julia Pfeiffer Burns State Park
℅ Pfeiffer Big Sur State Park
Big Sur, CA 93920
(408) 667-2315

Location

Julia Pfeiffer Burns State Park, located 37 miles south of Carmel on Highway 1, stretches from the legendary Big Sur coastline into nearby 3,000-foot ridges. The 3,543-acre park is in Monterey County.

Facilities & Activities

no regular campground
2 hike-in environmental campsites
no water
picnicking
hiking trails
designated underwater area

Special Notes

A unique feature of the park is a 1,680-acre underwater reserve protecting a spectacular assortment of marine life. Look for seals, sea lions, and playful sea otters in the cover. Other features include redwood, tan oak, madrone, chaparral, and an 80-foot waterfall that drops from granite cliffs right into the ocean.

The environmental campsites are in a cypress forest on the ocean bluffs overlooking the cove, with a spectacular view of the rugged coastline. These sites are subject to reservation. Check in at the Pfeiffer Big Sur State Park, 11 miles to the north on Highway 1. The sites are more than a mile from the parking lot and you must carry water.

Perhaps only an infinitesimal example of how the oceans were filled billions of years ago, 80-ft McWay Falls is still California's largest waterfall to fulfill its timeless goal.

Los Padres National Forest

For Information

Forest Supervisor
Los Padres National Forest
6144 Calle Real
Goleta, CA 93117
(805) 683-6711

Location

Los Padres National Forest, the third largest National Forest in California, covers almost two million acres. The forest is in two sections along the central coast. The main portion extends inland from coastal Santa Barbara and includes La Panza, Santa Ynez, San Rafael, and Sierra Madre Mountains. Farther north along the coast is the smaller section, which includes the Big Sur coast and Santa Lucia Mountains. The forest extends into six counties—Monterey, San Luis Obispo, Santa Barbara, Ventura, Kern, and Los Angeles.

The fire hazard in Los Padres National Forest is often extreme even though it is one of 3 national forests in the U.S. with ocean frontage.

Los Padres National Forest *(continued)*

Special Notes

Los Padres National Forest is a "land of contrast" in terms of terrain and climate. Daily temperatures inland can reach high and low extremes while conditions along the coast tend to be more moderate. When implemented, a "hazardous area fire closure" usually in effect from early July until mid-November affects much of the inland portion of the forest where the danger of wildfire is greatest.

Approximately 1,200 miles of trails offer numerous recreation opportunities for the hiker, backpacker, and equestrian. Fishing is a popular sport, especially in the springtime, along the more than 600 miles of fishing streams. The Mt. Pinos District offers the majority of cross-country skiing and snow-play opportunities, primarily on Mt. Pinos itself.

The Los Padres is unique in that it is one of three National Forests in the United States with ocean frontage. California's first designated Scenic Highway, SH 1, passes through a portion of the forest along the scenic Monterey County coastline. Two beach recreation areas are Pfeiffer Beach and Sand Dollar Beach, both day-use areas.

Ventana Wilderness marks the southernmost limit of the natural range of coastal redwoods.

Wilderness Areas

There are five Wilderness Areas within Los Padres National Forest. *The Ventana Wilderness* consists of 164,503 acres of rugged mountainous terrain, and lies within the heartlands of the Santa Lucia Mountains of Monterey County. This area contains the southernmost limit of the natural range of coast redwood. Waterfalls and deep pools can be found along major streams. Elevations range from 5,862 feet atop Junipero Sierra Peak to 600 feet along the Big Sur River.

The *Santa Lucia Wilderness* consists of 21,678 acres of streamside vegetation and chaparral-covered slopes surrounding Lopez Canyon. Elevation ranges from 800 feet along Lopez Creek to 3,000 feet in the vicinity of the Hi Mountain Lookout.

Machesna Mountain Wilderness consists of 20,000 acres located in the La Panza Mountain range. Elevations range from 1,600 feet to 4,063 feet atop Machesna Mountain. American Canyon is the major drainage.

The *San Rafael Wilderness* contains some 149,170 acres of mountainous country in the San Rafael and Sierra Madre Mountains. Elevations range from 1,166 to over 6,800 feet at Big Pine Mountain. The wilderness is open in the winter and spring months, but portions are closed in the summer and fall because of extreme fire danger. A 1,200-acre sanctuary for the California Condor is located within the Wilderness; entry is prohibited.

The *Dick Smith Wilderness* consists of 64,700 acres of extremely rugged topography with numerous canyons, some of which flow yearlong in their upper reaches. The area, 12 miles wide and 18 miles long, has elevations that range from 3,750 feet to 6,541 feet at the top of Madulce Peak. The wilderness contains a 7,680-acre critical habitat area of the California Condor.

Los Padres National Forest *(continued)*

Monterey Ranger District

Campground	Elevation (ft)	# of Units	Drinking Water	Toilets	Trailer Space	Fee Area
Arroyo Seco	900	46	*	V	*	*
Bottchers Gap	2,100	11	*	V		*
China Camp	4,500	6		V		*
Escondido	2,300	9	*	V	*	*
Kirk Creek	100	33	*	F	*	*
Memorial Park	2,000	8	*	V	*	*
Naciemento	1,600	8		V	*	*
Plaskett Creek	150	43	*	F	*	*
Ponderosa	1,500	23	*	V	*	*
White Oaks	4,000	7	*	F	*	*

Notes:
Campgrounds are open all year.
Bottchers Gap, China Camp and Escondido Campgrounds are trailhead campgrounds to Ventana Wilderness.
Memorial Park Campground is staging area for equestrian use of wilderness.
Arroyo Seco Campground has 1 group site for 50 persons at upper end of Abbott Lake; Plaskett Creek Campground has 3 group sites for 50 persons each at southern section; advance reservations required with Mistix.

For Information

Monterey Ranger District
406 South Mildred
King City, CA 93930
(408) 385-5434

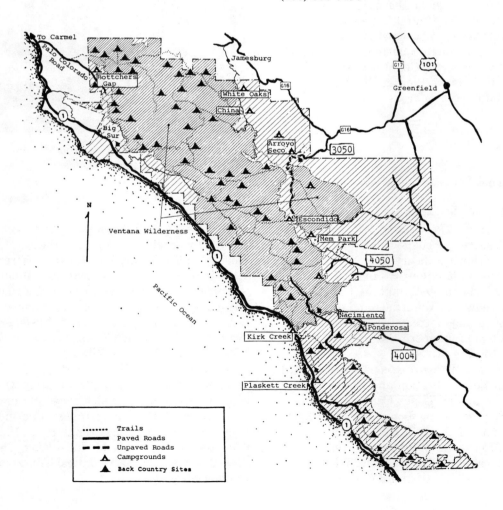

Los Padres National Forest *(continued)*

Santa Lucia Ranger District

Campgrounds	Elevation (ft)	# of Units	Drinking Water	Toilets	Trailer Space	Fee Area
American Canyon	1,700	14	spr.	V	*	
Aqua Escondido	2,200	3	*	V		
Barrel Springs	1,000	3	*	V		
Bates Canyon	2,700	6	spr.	V		
Brookshire Spring	1,500	2	*	V	*	
Cerro Alto	1,000	13	*	V	*	*
Colson Canyon	2,000	9	*	V		
Davy Brown	2,100	12	*	V		*
Figueroa	3,500	30	*	V		*
Hi Mountain	2,400	12	*	V		*
Horseshoe Spring	1,500	3	*	P		
La Panza	2,200	16	*	V		*
Miranda Pines	4,000	3		V		
Navajo	2,200	4	*	V		
Nira	2,000	6		V	*	
Queen Bee	2,400	4	spr.	V		
Stony Creek	1,800	12	spr.	V	*	
Wagon Flat	1,400	3		P		

Notes:
Nira Campground is trailhead to San Rafael Wilderness.
American Canyon, Aqua Escondido, and Stony Creek are open only in deer season.
6 campgrounds are open year-round: Bates Canyon, Cerro Alto, Hi Mountain, La Panza, Miranda Pines, and Navajo; others are open May 15–October 31.

For Information

Santa Lucia Ranger District
1616 Carlotti Drive
Santa Maria, CA 93454
(815) 925-9538

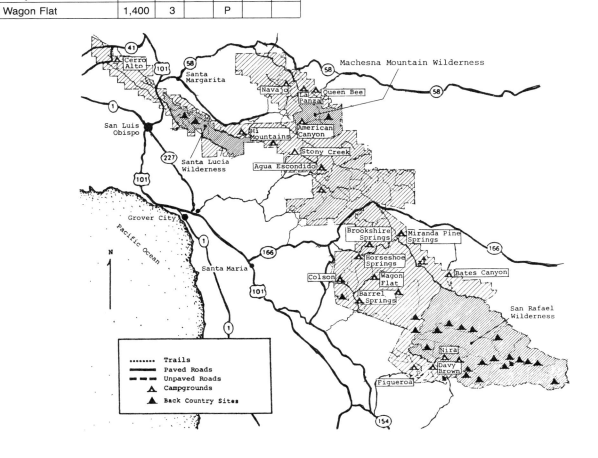

Los Padres National Forest (continued)

Santa Barbara Ranger District ——————

Campgrounds	Elevation (ft)	# of Units	Drinking Water	Toilets	Trailer Space	Fee Area
Cachuma	2,200	6	*	*		
Freemont	900	15	*	F	*	*
Juncal	1,800	6	*	*		
Los Prietos	1,000	37	*	F	*	
Middle Santa Ynez	1,800	3	*	*		
Mono	1,500	9		*		
Paradise	900	15	*	F	*	*
P-Bar Flat	1,800	3		*		
Red Rock	1,100	27		*	*	
Santa Ynez	1,100	34	*	*	*	*
Upper Oso	1,100	20		F		

Notes:

Paradise Campground has 2 group campsites; Sage Hill has group camping; facilities include drinking water and flush toilets, fee charged; advance reservations required through Mistix.

Campgrounds are open year-round, except Cachuma, and it is open April–December.

High river flow on Santa Ynez River often blocks road in winter to Red Rock, Santa Ynez, and Upper Oso campgrounds.

Sometimes after a long day's drive, even a parking lot with a picnic table provides a welcome respite.

For Information

Santa Barbara Ranger District
Star Route, Los Prietos
Santa Barbara, CA 93105
(805) 967-3481

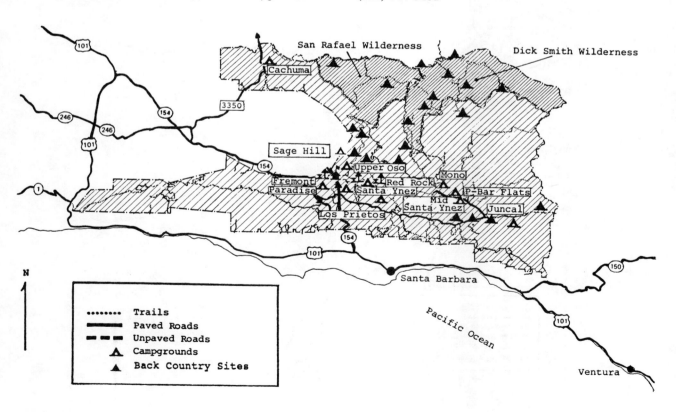

San Rafael Wilderness

Dick Smith Wilderness

Cachuma

Sage Hill

Upper Oso

Mono

Fremont
Paradise

Red Rock

P-Bar Flats

Santa Ynez

Mid
Santa Ynez

Juncal

Los Prietos

Santa Barbara

Pacific Ocean

Ventura

N

•••••••	Trails
——	Paved Roads
– – –	Unpaved Roads
△	Campgrounds
▲	Back Country Sites

Los Padres National Forest *(continued)*

Mt. Pinos Ranger District

Campgrounds	Elevation (ft)	# of Units	Drinking Water	Toilets	Trailer Space	Fee Area
Aliso	3,200	10		*	*	
Ballinger	3,000	5		*		
Camp Caballo	5,800	5		*	*	
Campo Alto	8,200	12	*		*	
Chuchupate	6,200	30	spr.	*	*	
Dome Spring	4,800	4		*		
Dutchman	6,800	9		*		
Halfmoon	4,700	10		*	*	
Hard Luck	2,800	4		*		
Hog Pen Springs	3,700	7	*	P		
Kings Camp	4,250	7		*		
Lockwood Creek	4,600	5		*		
Marian	6,600	5		P		
McGill	7,400	78	spr.	*	*	
Mt. Pinos	7,800	19	spr.	*	*	
Nettle Spring	4,400	9	*	*		
Ozena Camp	3,600	12	*	*	*	
Pine Springs	5,800	12		*		
Rancho Nuevo	3,600	2				
Reyes Creek	4,000	29	*	*		*
Thorn Meadows	5,000	4		*		
Tinta	3,600	3		*		

Notes:

5 campgrounds are open year-long: Aliso, Camp Alto, Dome Spring, Kings Camp and Ozena Camp; others are open April/May—Oct./Nov.

Ballinger Campground is used mainly by motorcyclists.

McGill Group Camp has 2 group sites: one has 80-person/18-car maximum; contact ranger district for details on other; fee charged, piped spring water, toilets; advance reservations required through Mistix.

For Information

Mt. Pinos Ranger District
Star Route, Box 400
Frazier Park, CA 93225
(805) 245-3731

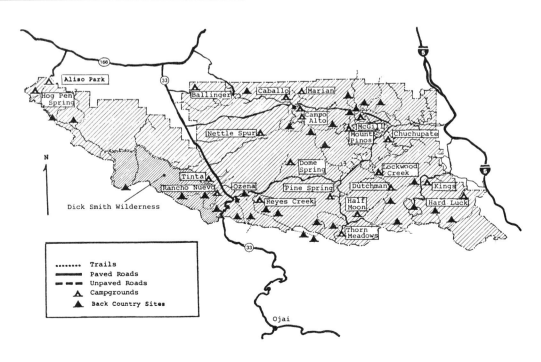

Los Padres National Forest *(continued)*

Ojai Ranger District

Campgrounds	Elevation (ft)	# of Units	Drinking Water	Toilets	Trailer Space	Fee Area
Beaver Camp	3,000	13	river	*	*	
Blue Point	1,000	43	*	*	*	*
Cherry Creek	4,500	2	str.			
Lion Canyon	3,000	30	*	*	*	*
Middle Lion	3,300	9	str.	P	*	
Pine Mountain	6,700	6	spr.	*		
Reyes Peak	6,800	6	spr.	*		
Rose Valley	3,400	9	*	P	*	*
Wheeler Gorge	1,900	73	*	F/P	*	*

Notes:

Holiday Group Campground requires advance reservations through Mistix; no fee; open year round; has pit toilets and water.

Spring water is available ¼-mile down trail at Raspberry Spring for Pine Mountain and Reyes Peak campgrounds.

Campgrounds are open year-round, except Lion Canyon, which is open April—Nov.

For Information

Ojai Ranger District
1190 East Ojai Avenue
Ojai, CA 93023
(805) 646-4348

California's Coastal Highway, U.S. 1, offers a different vista with each turn, but be alert, some of the vistas are steep and deep!

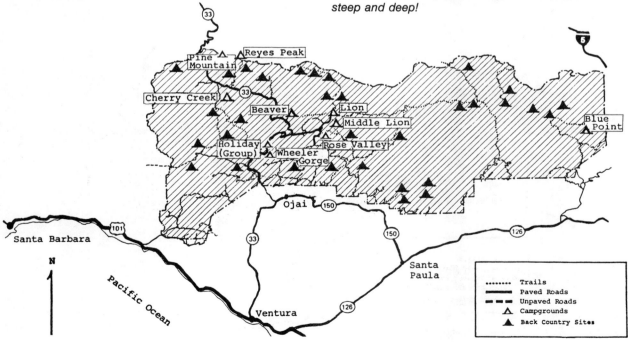

Morro Bay Area State Parks

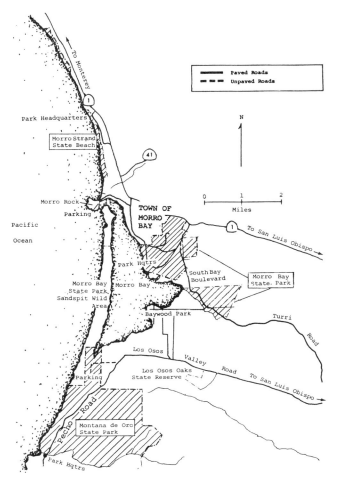

"Morro" is the Spanish term for a crown-shaped rock or hill. The 576-foot high rock at the entrance to Morro Bay is a plug dome volcanic outcropping, one of 9, and the northernmost of the volcanic peaks in a line between Morro Bay and San Luis Obispo. The climate in the Morro Bay area is very mild in winter and cool in summer, with considerable coastal fog between the first of June and the end of August. There is 1 state beach and 2 state parks in the Morro Bay area that have camping facilities and offer a wide variety of recreational opportunities: Morro Strand State Beach, Montana de Oro State Park, and Morro Bay State Park. For a recorded message, phone: (805) 772-2560.

Morro Strand State Beach

For Information

Morro Strand State Beach
% Morro Bay State Park
Morro Bay, CA 93442
(805) 772-2560

Location

Morro Strand State Beach (formerly Atascadero State Beach) is located west of Highway 1 between Yerba Buena Avenue and Atascadero Road on the north side of the city of Morro Bay. This 83-acre state beach has 1.7 miles of beach frontage, making it a popular place for walking along the shore and for beachcombing. The beach, which faces Estero Bay and the Pacific, is about a mile north of Morro Rock.

Facilities & Activities

104 developed campsites
outdoor cold showers
24-foot trailers; 24-foot campers/motorhomes
fishing
swimming
on State Park Reservation System (mid May—Aug.)

Montana de Oro State Park

For Information

Montana de Oro State Park
Pecho Road
Los Osos, CA 93402
(805) 528-0513

Location

Montana de Oro State Park is located 7 miles south of Los Osos on Pecho Road. The 7,328-acre park has rugged cliffs, secluded sandy beaches, coastal plains, 2 year-round streams in wooded canyons, chaparral-covered hills dotted with coastal live oak and Bishop pine, and 1,347-foot Valencia Peak. The park also has more than 1.5 miles of scenic shoreline.

Facilities & Activities

50 primitive campsites along Islay Creek
no showers
environmental campsites
enroute campsites
24-foot trailers; 24-foot campers/motorhomes
2 group camps—on State Park Reservation
  System (all year)
  Hazard Horse Group #1 and #2—each with
    50-person/12-vehicle max.; primitive; no
    showers; 31-foot vehicles; Group Camp #1 and
    #2 can be reserved together
picnicking
fishing
hiking trails (50 miles)
nature trail
horseback riding trails
equestrian camping (maximum of 25 horses and
  minimum of 7 horses); corrals; water troughs;
  trailer in; primitive camping; no showers—at
  Hazard Horse Group Camp
Islay Creek Campground on State Park
  Reservation System (mid-May—Aug.)

This park gets its name—mountain of gold—from the millions of wildflowers that bloom in spring.

Trails
Abandoned or Fireroads
(closed to public vehicles)
Park Service Roads
Paved and Parking Areas
Restrooms
Designated Horse Trails (1974)

Collecting Natural Features Prohibited

Morro Bay State Park

For Information

Morro Bay State Park
Morro Bay, CA 93442
(805) 772-2560

Location

Morro Bay State Park is in Morro Bay. The 2,435-acre park's entrances are 1 mile south of Highway 1 on South Bay Blvd. and at the south end of Main St. in Morro Bay. At the mouth of Los Osos Creek, an extensive marsh opens out into Morro Bay. A haven for countless birds, this is one of the largest natural areas of marshland still remaining anywhere along the coast of California.

Facilities & Activities

115 developed campsites
campsites for disabled
showers
31-foot trailers; 31-foot campers/motorhomes
20 hookup sites (water & electricity only) for
   31-foot trailers and 35-foot campers/motorhomes
enroute campsites
trailer sanitation station
2 group camps at Chorro Willows—on State Park
   Reservation System (all year); 1 site with 50
   person/25 vehicle max., 36-foot length max.; 1
   site with 30 person/15 vehicle max., 27-foot
   length max.; developed; shower facilities in

nearby campground; campsites may be reserved
   together
picnicking
group picnicking area (50 max.)
fishing
hiking trails
swimming
nature trails
exhibits
boating (launch ramp for small boats only,
   mooring, rentals)
food service
on State Park Reservation System (all year)

Morro Rock, a plug dome volcanic outcropping, is the nesting ground for many kinds of birds, including peregrine falcons.

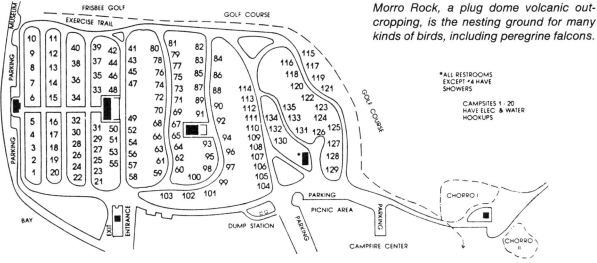

*ALL RESTROOMS
EXCEPT #4 HAVE
SHOWERS

CAMPSITES 1 - 20
HAVE ELEC & WATER
HOOKUPS

New Brighton State Beach

For Information

New Brighton State Beach
1500 Park Avenue and Highway 1
Capitola, CA 95010
(408) 475-4850
831-464 6330

Location

New Brighton State Beach is located 4 miles south of Santa Cruz on Highway 1. The 94-acre beach, in Santa Cruz County, is one of several Monterey Bay state beaches.

Facilities & Activities

115 developed campsites including 15 walk-in sites
campsites for disabled
showers
31-foot trailers; 31-foot campers/motorhomes
trailer sanitation station
enroute campsites
picnicking
fishing
swimming
on State Park Reservation System (April—Oct.)
Reserve America: 1 800 444-7275

Special Notes

8 people per site

The climate is favorable in the Monterey Bay area. The day's high temperature seldom rises

above 75° in the summer or drops below 60° in the winter. Surfers enjoy the bay's relatively warm waters, and they may use any of the beaches with due regard for other swimmers.

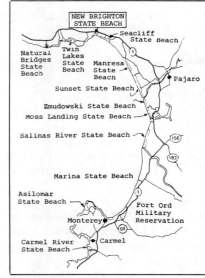

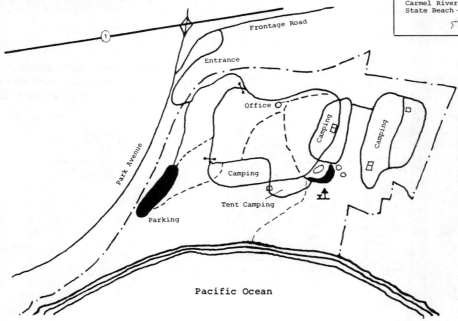

Pfeiffer Big Sur State Park

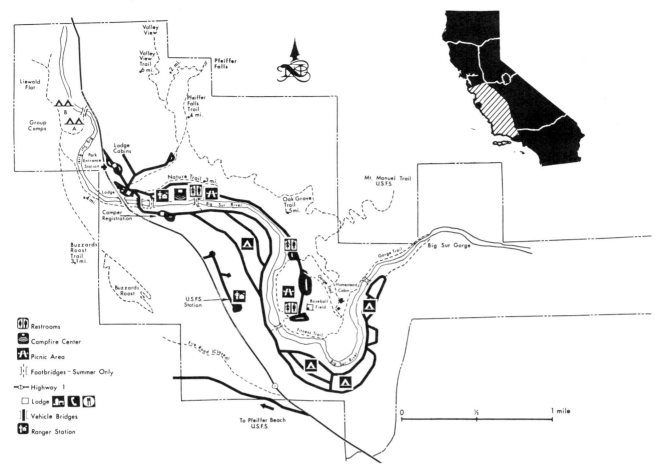

Restrooms
Campfire Center
Picnic Area
Footbridges – Summer Only
Highway 1
Lodge
Vehicle Bridges
Ranger Station

For Information

Pfeiffer Big Sur State Park
Big Sur, CA 93920
(408) 667-2315

Location

Pfeiffer Big Sur State Park, in Monterey County, is located 26 miles south of Carmel on Highway 1. The elevation of the park is 215 feet, although the mountains in the vicinity of the 821-acre park, part of the Santa Lucia Mountain Range, rise to a maximum of 3,700 feet.

Facilities & Activities

217 developed campsites
campsites for disabled
showers
27-foot trailers; 32-foot campers/motorhomes
trailer sanitation station
2 group camping areas (max. 50 each); open
  Memorial Day—Sept.
picnicking
group picnicking area (200 max.)
fishing
6 hiking trails
swimming
nature trails
exhibits
food service
supplies
concession operated motel-type cabins
on State Park Reservation System (all year)

Special Notes

Though the park has no direct ocean access, the ocean may be easily reached via Sycamore Canyon Road, one mile south of the park entrance or via Andrew Molera State Park, 4½ miles north. The eastern, or gorge, area of the park is bordered by the Ventana Wilderness with more than 200 miles of scenic hiking trails. The 6 trails in the park range from .3 to 4.0 miles, from 20 minutes to 2 hours in length.

Pinnacles National Monument

For Information

Superintendent
Pinnacles National Monument
Paicines, CA 95043
~~(408) 389-4578~~

(408) 389-4485

Directions:

101 South
25 Gilroy
continue south/east
towards Hollister
2½-3 HRS.

Campgrounds
  west-side — 18 sites $10.00 per site (6 people)
  east-side — 100 sites $6.00 per person/nite — cooler,
    hot showers, swimming pool.   more shade.

389-4462
M-F
  4:00-5:00
S-S
  9-5

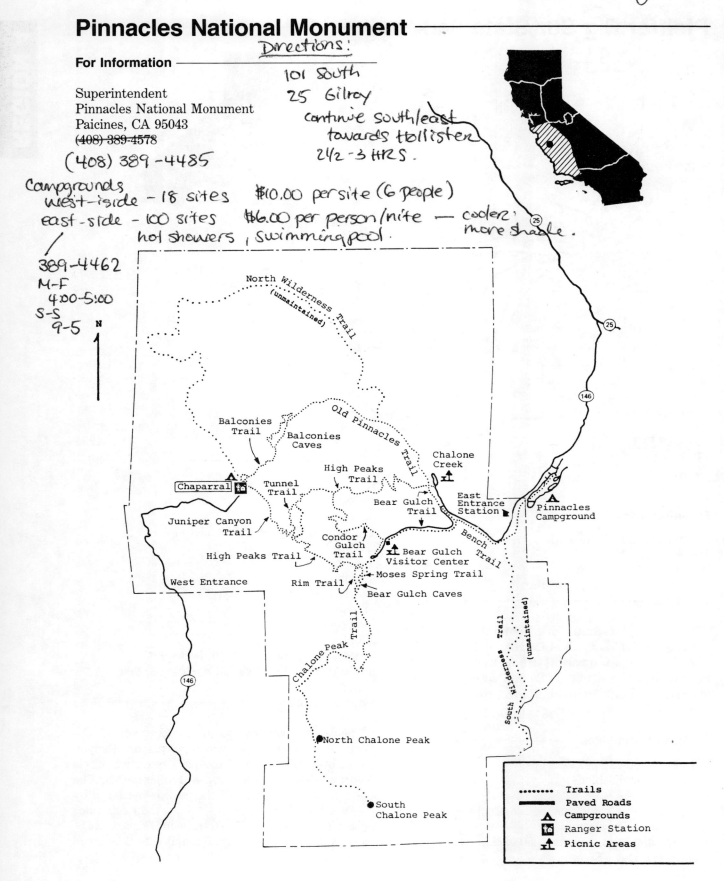

Pinnacles National Monument *(continued)*

Location

Pinnacles National Monument is located 150 miles south of San Francisco. It is a 16,221-acre rugged chaparral area containing rock pinnacles and spires created by erosion of an ancient volcano. Pinnacles has west and east entrances, but there is no through-road connecting the east and west sides. The east entrance to Bear Gulch Visitor Center and Chalone Creek picnic area is via SH 146 off of SH 25 some 30 miles south of Hollister. The west entrance to Chaparral Ranger Station and Campground is 12 miles on SH 146 from U.S. 101 at Soledad.

Facilities & Activities

24 walk-in campsites at Chaparral Campground; no trailers
campground phone number: (408) 389-4526
water and modern comfort stations
picnic tables
fireplaces
accessible to handicapped
camping fee charged
no reservations
no backcountry camping
picnicking

26 miles of hiking trails
self-guiding nature trails
cave touring
technical rock climbing
Bear Gulch Visitor Center (east)
Chaparral Ranger Station (west)

Special Notes

Jagged pinnacles, spires, and other towering rock formations 1,200 to 3,300 feet high rise above the smooth contours of the surrounding countryside. The park lies on the earthquake-prone San Andreas Fault. The park is open all year although the main travel seasons are during the fall and spring months. In July and August, the daytime temperatures may reach 100° or more and December through February are usually the wet months.

The road from Soledad to west Pinnacles is narrow; visitors driving large campers and towing trailers should use extreme caution. Technical rock climbing is a popular activity. Permits are not required, but climbers are advised to register with a park ranger before and after a climb. The caves have low ceilings and slippery rocks. Flashlights should be used.

In stark contrast to the jagged, vertical landscape of Pinnacles National Monument is this flat, very horizontal farmland nearby.

Pismo Dunes State Vehicular Recreation Area

For Information

Pismo Dunes State Vehicular Recreation Area
576 Camino Mercado
Arroyo Grande, CA 93420
(805) 473-7220

Location

Pismo Dunes State Vehicular Recreation Area is located 3 miles south of the city of Pismo Beach on Highway 1 with access to the beach via Pier Avenue. The 2,500-acres of sand dunes located in San Luis Obispo County are used by off-road vehicles.

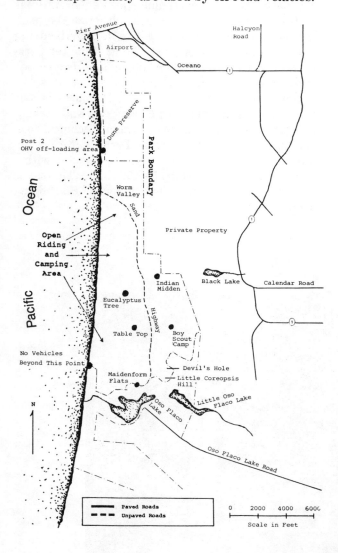

Four-wheelers have a 2,500-acre playground at Pismo Dunes State Vehicular Recreation Area.

Facilities & Activities

primitive camping on beach; no designated sites
recommended for 4-wheel drive only
limited to 500 camping units
chemical toilets
bring own water; pack out own trash
no showers
40-foot trailers; 40-foot campers/motorhomes
on State Park Reservation System (all year)
picnicking
fishing
hiking
horseback riding

Special Notes

This sand dune complex is geologically unique and also provides an impressive playground for off-highway enthusiasts from throughout the United States. High tides, heavy rains, and blowing sand determine whether or not you can drive down the beach without getting stuck. Post #2 is 1 mile south on the beach from Pier Avenue and marks the beginning of the off-road vehicle area. All off-road vehicles must be transported to this point before off-loading.

Pismo State Beach

For Information

Pismo State Beach
555 Pier Avenue
Oceano, CA 93445
(805) 489-2684

Location

Pismo State Beach runs for a distance of approximately 7 miles, from the foot of Wilmar Street in the city of Pismo Beach to the county line at the Santa Maria River. This 1,051-acre beach is in San Luis Obispo County south of the city on Highway 1.

The North Beach Campground is located 300 yards from the ocean, separated by sand dunes and eucalyptus groves. It is on Highway 1, Dolliver Street, in Pismo Beach. Oceano Campground is on Pier Avenue off Highway 1 in Oceano.

Facilities & Activities

185 developed campsites
North Beach Campground:
    103 developed sites (no hookups)
    no showers
    sanitation station
    31-foot trailers; 36-foot campers/motorhomes
    on State Park Reservation System
        (mid-May—mid-Sept.)
Oceano Campground:
    42 sites with hookups (electricity/water only)

40 sites without hookups
showers
campsites for hikers/bicyclists
31-foot trailers/36-foot campers/motorhomes for
    hookup sites
18-foot trailers/31-foot campers/motorhomes for
    other sites
on State Park Reservation System (all year)
picnicking
fishing
hiking

Special Notes

Most people who visit Pismo State Beach participate in some form of water sport—surf fishing, SCUBA and skin diving, sand castle building, wading, and especially clamming. The abundance of Pismo clams in its tidal waters has made Pismo State Beach famous. Pismo is the only beach in California where the sand is firm enough to support travel by standard highway automobiles, and where this activity is permitted. The weather is moderate year-round, with an average temperature of 60° summer and winter. Summers tend to be foggy, and winters, clear and windy. Water temperatures both summer and winter are cold, often less than 58°.

Facing water temperatures of 58° or less, it's possible this diver is having second thoughts.

Portola State Park

For Information

Portola State Park
Star Route 2
La Honda, CA 94020
(415) 948-9098

Location

Portola State Park is located 7 miles southwest of Skyline Boulevard (Highway 35) off of Alpine Road in southern San Mateo County. The 2,400-acre park has an elevation of 450 feet.

Facilities & Activities

52 developed campsites
showers
24-foot trailers; 27-foot campers/motorhomes
walk-in trail camp (3 miles)
2 group camping areas: Circle Group Camp and Point Group Camp; (each 50 person/12 vehicle max.); on State Park Reservation System, all year; developed; no showers; tents only; 50-yard walk; can be reserved together for group of 100; no RVs in lot
picnicking
group picnicking area (parking for 35 vehicles)
hiking trails (14 miles)
nature trail
exhibits
on State Park Reservation System (all year)

Special Notes

This park has a rugged, natural basin forrested with coast redwoods, Douglas fir, and live oak. Miles of trails crisscross the deep canyon and its two streams, Peters Creek and Pescadero Creek. The development of Pescadero Creek County Park has opened 7,000 acres of hiking and equestrian trails to the west. Visitors are invited to explore this combined area during any time of the year.

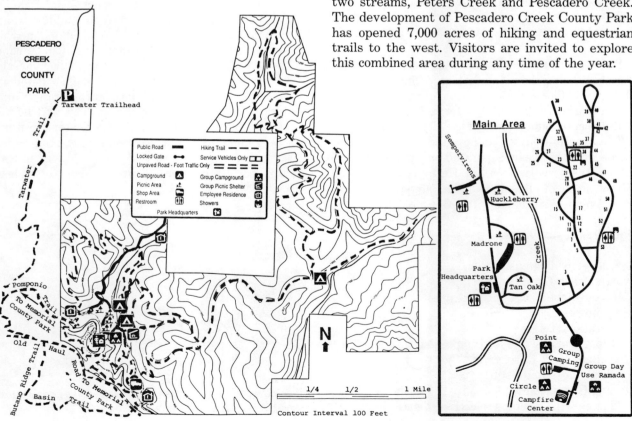

San Luis Reservoir State Recreation Area

For Information

San Luis Reservoir State Recreation Area
31426 West Highway 152
Santa Nella, CA 95322
(209) 826-1196

Location

San Luis Reservoir State Recreation Area is nestled in the grassy hills on the west side of the San Joaquin Valley near historic Pacheco Pass. Water arrives at the reservoir via the California Aqueduct and the Delta-Mendota Canal. Since San Luis is a storage reservoir, the lake level drops throughout the summer. Located in Merced County, 12 miles west of Los Banos on Highway 152, the 26,026-acre park has an elevation of 400 feet above sea level.

Facilities & Activities

3 campgrounds
79 developed campsites at Basalt Campground at
  San Luis Reservoir
  solar showers
  campsites for disabled
  trailer sanitation station
  37-foot trailers; 37-foot campers/motorhomes
  on State Park Reservation System
    (mid-March—mid-Sept.)
38 primitive campsites at Medeiros Area at
  O'Neil Forebay
  maximum of 500 overflow sites without grills
    and tables

  drinking water only
  chemical toilets
20 primitive campsites at Los Banos Creek
  Reservoir
  drinking water only
  chemical toilets
  camping area designated for horsemen
picnicking
fishing
swimming
exhibits
horseback riding at Los Banos Creek Reservoir
boating (launch ramp, water skiing, sailing)

Special Notes

A section of the California Aqueduct Bikeway begins at the San Luis Creek area and heads toward Bethany Reservoir near Livermore, 70 miles to the north. The bikeway has rest stops at 10-mile intervals. San Luis Reservoir has a surface area of 14,000 acres, while O'Neil Forebay has 2,000 surface acres and Los Banos has 400 surface acres.

Be aware that length restrictions for camper/motorhomes/trailers vary from park to park.

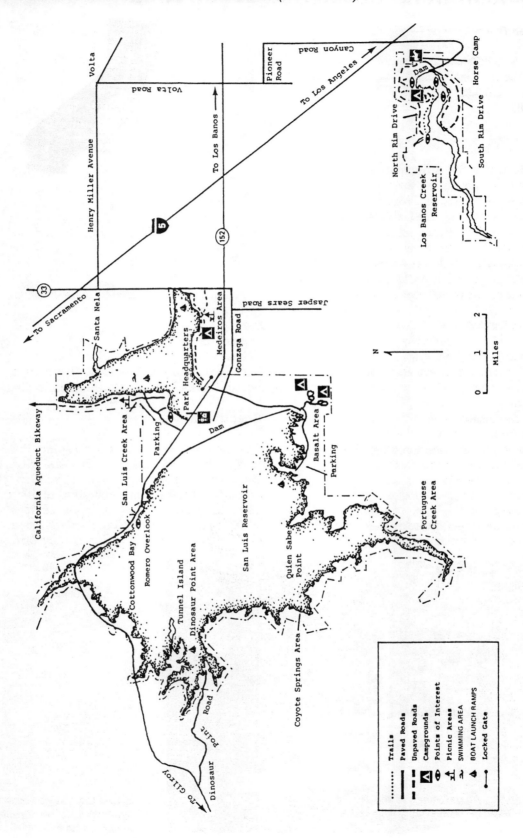

San Simeon State Beach

For Information

San Simeon State Beach
750 Hearst Castle Rd.
San Simeon, CA 93452
(805) 927-2020

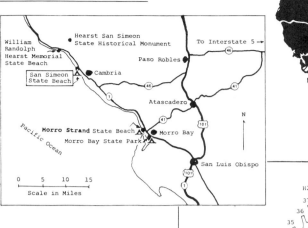

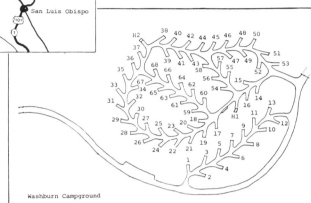

Washburn Campground

Location

San Simeon State Beach is located 5 miles south of San Simeon on Highway 1. The 541-acre state beach, in San Luis Obispo County, is at sea level. The beach is west of Highway 1 and the campground is east of Highway 1 with beach access underneath the Highway 1 San Simeon Creek overpass.

Facilities & Activities

2 campgrounds: San Simeon Creek and Washburn
130 developed campsites at San Simeon
    approximately 40 of these for tents only
    solar showers
    handicapped accessible
    31-foot trailers/campers/motorhomes
70 primitive sites at Washburn
    chemical toilets
    handicapped accessible
    no showers
picnicking
fishing
on State Park Reservation System
    (mid-March—Sept.)

Special Notes

San Simeon Creek provides steelhead fishing during the winter season and a myriad of nature activities for the summer visitors. Numerous interpretive programs are scheduled throughout the summer season.

Nearby San Simeon State Beach is the Hearst San Simeon State Historical Monument—America's "Taj Mahal."

Santa Barbara County State Beaches

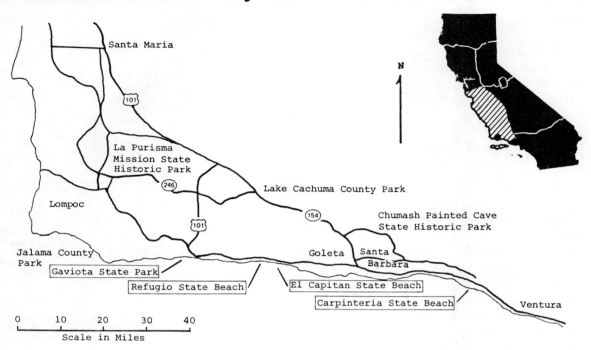

Santa Barbara County has 3 state beaches and 1 state park on the beach that offers campgrounds—Carpinteria, El Capitan, Gaviota, and Refugio. These camping recreation areas are located on a long stretch of coast that faces south and is sheltered from large waves by the northern Channel Islands, located 20 to 30 miles to the south. The sandy beaches, known for good swimming, are bordered to the north by the scenic mountains of the Santa Ynez range, characterized by steep-walled canyons and sharp peaks that vary in elevation from 1,500 to 4,000 feet. These mountains are unique in California for their east-west orientation.

Sprawling, sandy beaches that appeal to swimmers and surfers typify Santa Barbara County State Beaches.

Refugio State Beach

For Information

Refugio State Beach
#10 Refugio Beach Road
Goleta, CA 93117
(805) 968-3294

Location

Refugio State Beach is located 23 miles northwest of Santa Barbara on U.S. 101. This 155-acre park, located close to the ocean, is one of the more complete beaches near Santa Barbara and has superb coastal fishing.

Facilities & Activities

85 developed campsites
campsites for disabled
showers
30-foot trailers; 30-foot campers/motorhomes

group camping area (60 person/20 vehicle, including trailers, max.) on State Park Reservation System (mid-April—Dec.); primitive; no showers; 21-foot max.; may be closed by spring and fall rains
picnicking
fishing
hiking trail
swimming
food service
supplies
on State Park Reservation System (mid-April—Dec.)

Gaviota, Spanish for sea gull, is a popular year-round park.

Gaviota State Park

For Information

Gaviota State Park
#10 Refugio Beach Road
Goleta, CA 93117
(805) 968-1711

Location

Gaviota State Park, 2,776 acres, is located 33 miles west of Santa Barbara on U.S. 101. The park is close to the ocean.

Facilities & Activities

38 RV sites
19 tent sites
campsites for disabled
showers
30-foot trailers; 30-foot campers/motorhomes
picnicking
fishing
hiking
swimming
horseback riding trail
boating (launching hoist on fishing pier; provide own slings; 3-ton limit)
food service
supplies
on State Park Reservation System (all year)

The fishing pier at Gaviota State Park has a 3-ton boat launch.

El Capitan State Beach

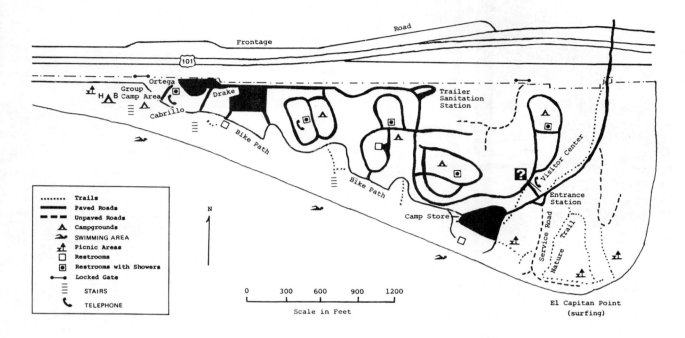

Trails
Paved Roads
Unpaved Roads
Campgrounds
SWIMMING AREA
Picnic Areas
Restrooms
Restrooms with Showers
Locked Gate
STAIRS
TELEPHONE

0   300   600   900   1200

Scale in Feet

El Capitan Point
(surfing)

Hot-blooded, cold-blooded, or somewhere in between, California beaches attract all sorts of folks.

For Information

El Capitan State Beach
#10 Refugio Beach Road
Goleta, CA 93117
(805) 968-3294

Location

El Capitan State Beach is located 20 miles northwest of Santa Barbara on U.S. 101. The 133-acre park has 9,450 feet of well developed beach with 3.5 miles of bike trails. The campsites are situated along 4 loop roads and all are within a few minutes walk to the beach.

Facilities & Activities

140 developed campsites
campsites for disabled
showers
27-foot trailers; 30-foot campers/motorhomes
trailer sanitation station
campsites for hikers/bicyclists
3 group camps—on State Park Reservation
    System (all year); developed; tent camping only;

Santa Barbara County State Beaches *(continued)*

50–100 yard walk-in
   Cabrillo (75 person/15 vehicle max.)
   Drake (125 person/25 vehicle max.)
   Ortega (50 person/10 vehicle max.)
picnicking
fishing

hiking trail
swimming
nature trail
food service
supplies
on State Park Reservation System (all year)

Carpinteria State Beach

For Information

Carpinteria State Beach
24 East Main Street
Ventura, CA 93001
(805) 684-2811

Location

Carpinteria State Beach is located 12 miles south of Santa Barbara off U.S. 101; take Carpinteria Street exit to Palm Avenue. This 50-acre park has 4,000 feet of ocean frontage, and is a narrow beach bordered by a dune area on the east side and by a bluff on the west. The beach is known as the "safest beach on the coast" because of the shallow offshore shelf.

Facilities & Activities

4 campgrounds: Anacapa, Santa Cruz, Santa Rosa and San Miguel
campsites for disabled
showers
on State Park Reservation System (all year)
172 developed campsites
86 full hookup campsites

campground specifics:
   101 sites at Anacapa and Santa Cruz—tents; motorhomes up to 30 feet; no hookups; no trailers
   157 sites at Santa Rosa and San Miguel— trailers up to 22 feet; motorhomes up to 30 feet; no tents; full hookup sites at Santa Rosa only
trailer sanitation station
picnicking
fishing
swimming
supplies

Recreation, meditation, and inspiration are all possible on peaceful Carpinteria State Beach.

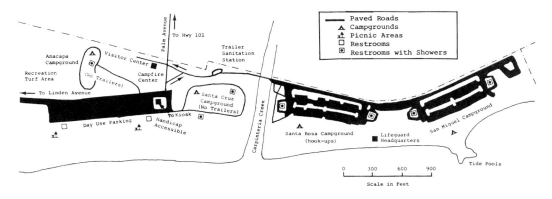

Seacliff State Beach

Beachcombing is fun because it always offers the hope of finding something.

For Information

Seacliff State Beach
Highway 1 & State Park Drive
Aptos, CA 95003
(408) 688-3222

Location

Seacliff State Beach is located 5½ miles south of Santa Cruz on Highway 1. It is in Santa Cruz County and is 85 acres in size.

Facilities & Activities

26 full hook-up sites
campsites for disabled
showers
36-foot trailers; 40-foot campers/motorhomes
picnicking
fishing
swimming
exhibits
food service
on State Park Reservation System (April—Dec.)

Special Notes

This state beach is favored for the fishing pier and concrete ship. It's a good location for swimming and the surfing is ideal. The climate is favorable as the day's high temperature seldom rises above 75° in the summer or drops below 60° in the winter.

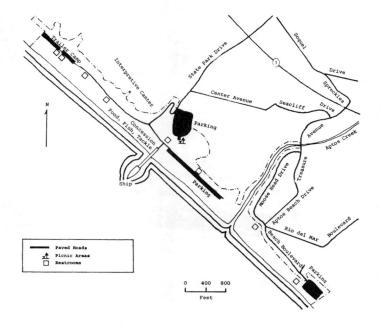

Sunset State Beach

For Information

Sunset State Beach
201 Sunset Beach Road
Watsonville, CA 95076
(408) 688-3241

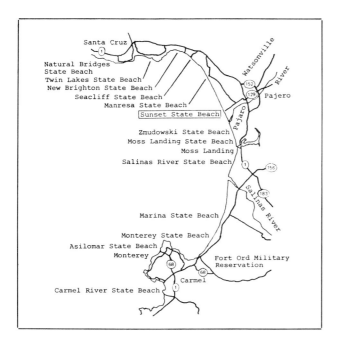

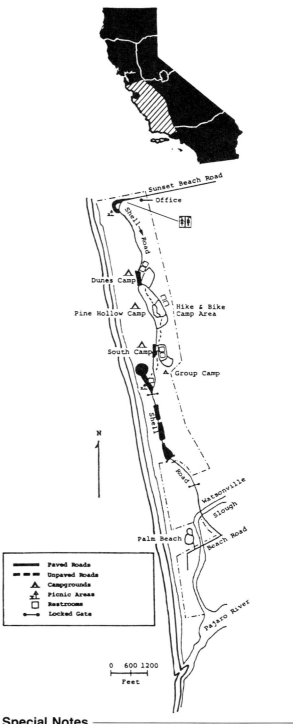

Location

Sunset State Beach is located 16 miles south of Santa Cruz via Highway 1 and San Andreas Road. The 324-acre state beach is in Santa Cruz County.

Facilities & Activities

90 developed campsites
campsites for disabled
showers
31-foot trailers; 31-foot campers/motorhomes
group camping area (50 person/10 vehicle max.)—on State Park Reservation System (all year); developed; showers; limit 2 RVs per group; 18-foot max.; tent camping only
picnicking
fishing
food service
on State Park Reservation System (April—mid-Sept.)

Special Notes

The campgrounds at Sunset State Beach sit on the bluffs above the beach. This is a favorite spot for seekers of the Pismo clam. Clam diggers should beware, however, of heavy surf, riptides, and the uneven bottom.

REGION 5

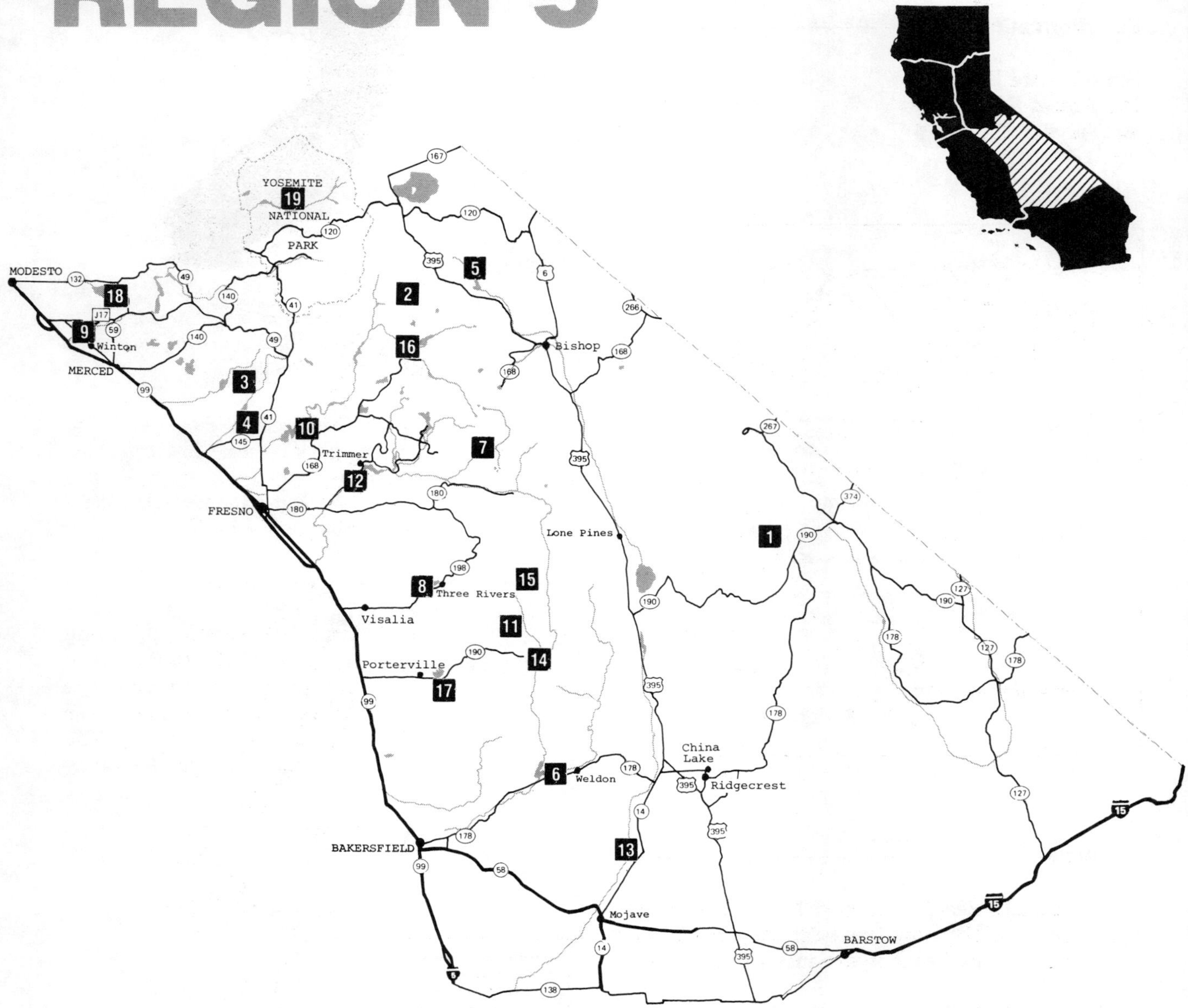

YOSEMITE
19
NATIONAL
PARK

MODESTO
18
9 Winton
MERCED
3
4
10 Trimmer
12
FRESNO
2
16
Bishop
5
7
Lone Pines
1
8 Three Rivers
Visalia
15
11
Porterville
14
17
6 Weldon
China Lake
Ridgecrest
BAKERSFIELD
13
Mojave
BARSTOW

1—Death Valley National Monument, 49
2—Devils Postpile National Monument, 52
3—Eastman Lake, 53
4—Hensley Lake, 54
5—Inyo National Forest, 55
6—Isabella Lake, 61
7—Kings Canyon National Park, 62
8—Lake Kaweah, 65
9—McConnell State Recreation Area, 66
10—Millerton Lake State Recreation Area, 67

11—Mountain Home State Forest, 69
12—Pine Flat Lake, 70
13—Red Rock Canyon State Park, 71
14—Sequoia National Forest, 72
15—Sequoia National Park, 79
16—Sierra National Forest, 83
17—Success Lake, 89
18—Turlock Lake State Recreation Area, 90
19—Yosemite National Park, 91

Death Valley National Monument

The hottest spot in North America is in Death Valley (see page 51 for the annual temperature range).

For Information

Superintendent
Death Valley National Monument
Death Valley, CA 92328
(619) 786-2331

Location

Death Valley National Monument is located east of Sequoia National Park near the Nevada border. U.S. 395 passes west of Death Valley and connects with SH 178 and SH 190 to the park. U.S. 95 passes east and connects with Nevada SH 267, SH 374, and SH 373 to the park. I-15 passes southeast and connects with SH 127. The park is more than 1½ times the size of Delaware, encompassing more than 2 million acres. Elevations range from 282 feet below sea level to 11,049 feet.

Special Notes

Nearly surrounded by high mountains, this large desert contains the lowest point in the western hemisphere. The area includes Scotty's Castle, the palatial home of a famous prospector, and other remnants of gold and borax mining activity. The name is foreboding and gloomy, yet in the valley

REGION 5

North Half

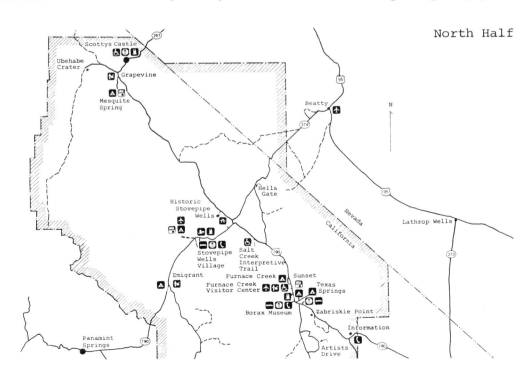

South Half

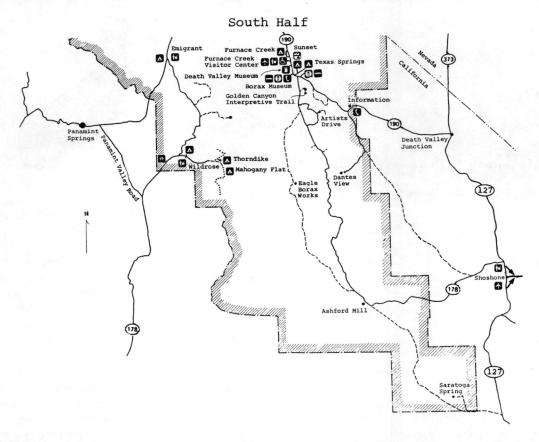

CAMPGROUNDS	ELEVATION	SEASON	SITES	FEE $	WATER	TABLES	FIRE-PLACES	FLUSH TOILETS	PIT TOILETS	SANITARY STATION
FURNACE CREEK	-196 feet	all yr.	156	X	X	X	X	X	X	X
TEXAS SPRING	sea level	Nov.-Apr.	93	X	X	X	X	X	X	X
SUNSET	-190 feet	Nov.-Apr.	1000	X	X		NO FIRES	X	X	X
STOVE PIPE WELLS	sea level	Nov.-Apr.	200	X	X		NO FIRES	X		X
EMIGRANT	2100 feet	Apr.-Oct.	10		X	X	X	X		
MESQUITE SPRING	1800 feet	all yr.	53††	X	X	X	X	X		X
WILDROSE	4100 feet	all yr.	36			X	X		X	
THORNDIKE*	7500 feet	Mar.-Nov.	8			X	X		X	
MAHOGANY FLAT*	8200 feet	Mar.-Nov.	10†			X	X		X	
PINYON MESA*	6400 feet	Mar.-Nov.	2			2	X		X	

†Designated sites—One vehicle or camping unit only, per site.   *Road not passable for trailers, campers or motor homes. Passenger cars not advisable. 4-wheel drive may be necessary.
††Designated sites—Two vehicles or camping units only, per site.

CAMPING LIMIT 30 DAYS PER YEAR.   Fees collected all year.

and the surrounding mountains you can find spectacular wildflower displays, snow-covered peaks, beautiful sand dunes, abandoned mines, and the hottest spot in North America.

Death Valley's size and the distances between its major features make the use of an automobile essential. Travelers should make sure their car is in good mechanical condition and that the fuel tank is full before beginning each day's tour. The park has several hundred miles of roads, including unpaved roads suitable for ordinary cars. There is also a network of primitive roads, but these are unsafe except for four-wheel-drive vehicles. All vehicles, including four-wheel drive and trail bikes, must stay on established roads.

On any given day, the valley floor shimmers silently in the heat. The air is clear and the sky is a deep blue. Six months of the year unmerciful heat

Death Valley National Monument *(continued)*

A harsh, forbidding environment, Death Valley is also a place of stark and unique beauty.

dominates the scene; for the next six months the heat releases its grip only slightly. Rain rarely gets past the guardian mountains. The animals that live in the desert are mainly nocturnal, for once the sun sets, the temperature falls quickly because of the dry air. Larger animals, such as the desert bighorn, live in the cooler, higher elevations. With height, moisture increases, until on the high peaks there are forests with juniper, mountain mahogany, pinyon, and other pines. And often the peaks surrounding the valley are snow-covered.

From June through September daytime temperatures are commonly in the 100+°F range; the rest of the year highs range from the 60s to the 90s. If you travel in Death Valley in the summer, pick up the folder "Hot Weather Hints" at distribution boxes at any entrance to the park, at the visitor center, or at a ranger station. Death Valley's temperature and rainfall records are among the oddest in the country. These averages, from the park brochure, give you an idea of what to expect each month.

	Avg. high temp. (°F)	Avg. low temp. (°F)	Record high temp. (°F)	Avg. rainfall (in.)
Jan.	64.6	39.3	87	.22
Feb.	72.9	46.2	91	.33
March	80.8	53.9	101	.15
April	88.4	61.6	109	.12
May	99.5	71.4	120	.06
June	109.7	81.6	125	.02
July	116.2	88.5	134	.11
Aug.	113.5	85.5	126	.06
Sept.	106.0	77.8	120	.10
Oct.	91.3	61.9	110	.11
Nov.	75.4	48.4	97	.19
Dec.	65.9	40.3	86	.19

Facilities & Activities

7 campgrounds for tents and RVs with 1,548 campsites (see chart)

3 backcountry campsites, for hike-in and 4-wheel drive, with 20 tent sites (see chart)

2 group campgrounds; reservations required, contact park

Mesquite Spring: open all year, 1 site for 35 persons/8 vehicles

Texas Spring: open Nov.—April; 1 site for 150 persons/10 vehicles; 1 site for 50 persons/10 vehicles

camp only in designated campgrounds; no roadside camping permitted; first-come, first-served basis, no reservations

backcountry travel allowed for those properly prepared; check with rangers

picnicking

hiking

self-guiding interpretive trails

auto touring

bicycling/bicycle rentals

jeep and 4-wheel drive touring

horseback riding

ranger-guided walks/naturalist talks

guided Castle tour (fee)

Furnace Creek visitor center/audiovisual programs

museums/interpretive exhibits

2 resorts provide lodging and other commercial services:

Stovepipe Wells concessioner (services limited May—Oct.)

Furnace Creek Inn and Ranch (private)

snacks and gasoline at Scotty's Castle

campfires are permitted in designated campgrounds; supply own fuel

pets must be leashed at all times

collecting or disturbing any natural or historic feature is not allowed

Devils Postpile National Monument

For Information

Devils Postpile National Monument
P.O. Box 501
Mammoth Lakes, CA 93546
(209) 565-3134 (winter)
(619) 934-2289 (summer)

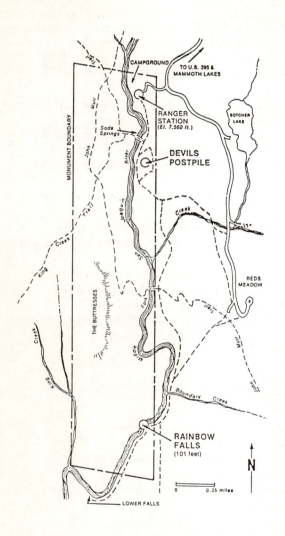

Facilities & Activities

23 campsites at Devils Postpile Campground
camping season: mid-June—Oct. 1, dependent on
    road and snow conditions
water and flush toilets
camping fee
no reservations
fishing
walk-in picnicking areas
hiking trails
evening ranger programs
road beyond Minaret Summit is closed to private
    vehicles in the summer; shuttle system available
    from Mammoth Lakes for day trips to the
    Monument; when camping in the valley, the
    camping permit allows you to drive to
    campground, then the shuttle can be used for
    short trips.

Location

Devils Postpile National Monument, just south-east of Yosemite, can be reached only from the east from U.S. 395 by a 10-mile drive to Minaret Summit on SH 203 through Mammoth Lakes, then by 7 miles of narrow mountain road. The 798-acre monument is at 7,600 feet elevation on the western slope of the Sierra Nevada, on the Middle Fork of the San Joaquin River.

Special Notes

The Devils Postpile is among the finest examples of columnar basalt in the world. One sheer wall of columns 60 feet high is exposed; many fallen columns now lie fragmented on the talus slope below. A second major feature of this region of the Sierra Nevada is the 101-foot-high Rainbow Falls. Hiking trails lead to both areas. The John Muir Trail between Yosemite and Kings Canyon National Parks crosses the monument. Bears inhabit the park, so proper food storage is required.

Each of the lakes in the Sierra Nevada has its own character and appeal, but all of them are beautiful.

A rocky, sprawling, diverse region, Anza-Borrego Desert State Park has lots of regular campsites, but it's also the only California state park where you can camp just about anywhere you want (page 104).

California's lakes, parks, forests, and beaches are truly playgrounds of discovery.

California offers such a variety of camping/hiking experiences that you can stroll through a desert one day and trek across a snow field the next.

The most colorful and least crowded time to visit Yosemite National Park is in the spring and fall (page 91).

Not exactly Class 4 rapids, but there are plenty of thrills to go around (page 73).

A fitting sunset for Orange County State Beaches (pages 123–125).

Yosemite Valley is magnificent, but don't forget it's only about 7 of the park's 1,200 square miles (page 91).

Wilderness areas in California's national forests offer "pure" camping opportunities in undeveloped, isolated, natural surroundings. No-trace camping practices should be observed (page I-11).

With fishing being so highly competitive it's a good idea to check out your competition.

Death Valley National Monument is a place of extremes: hottest temperatures, lowest dryland points, driest climate, and starkest beauty (page 49).

A dentist, schoolteacher, or mother of three during the week, she can "walk on the wild side" at California parks on weekends.

Four-wheelers might see Pismo Dunes State Vehicular Recreation Area (page 25) in this picture, and others might see Anza-Borrego Desert State Park (page 106). Which do you see?

The 60-foot "posts" of Devils Postpile National Monument are among the finest examples of columnar basalt in the world (page 52).

Don't forget your fishing gear when you go camping, because many streams in California parks are stocked with trout.

"I met a Californian who would
Talk California—a state so blessed
He said, in climate, none had ever died there,
a natural death."
        Robert Frost
        New Hampshire

An eagle's eye view of Sequoia National Park (page 79) . . .

He's got plenty of lean, but not enough wind to "fly the hull." (See page I-13 for information about California lakes.)

. . . and a one-of-a-kind group portrait.

On a clear day you can see forever.

The Pacific Crest National Park Scenic Trail covers 1,615 miles in California and any part of it offers challenge and beauty to match your pace and interest (page I-16).

R. Beelby

Calif. Dept. of Parks and Recreation

Even the desert comes alive after a rare spring rain.

More than half of Sequoia National Park is wilderness area, so chances are good you'll be able to camp by your very own lake (page 79).

R. Beelby

Calif. Dept. of Parks and Recreation

For the camper who prefers surf to turf, California has several state beaches that offer the best (pages 42–47, 123–125, 138–141).

While it may not look like it from here, the Golden Trout Wilderness of Inyo National Forest is a good area for novice backpackers (page 55).

It's a setting sun that makes these trees seem ablaze, but many of California's parks and forests are extremely susceptible to fires, so please be careful with all ignition sources.

In Inyo National Forest there is a bristlecone pine called Methuselah that is believed to be 4,600 years old (page 55).

Lakes in the Sierra Nevada are bluer than the sky and colder than . . . well, they're real cold.

A few of California's 840+ miles of coastline are not picture perfect like this, but don't worry, you probably won't even notice them.

Swimming, surfing, boating, and fishing are certainly the most popular water sports in California, but you can have a lot of fun under the water, too (pages 42–47, 123–125, 138–141).

Eastman Lake

For Information

Corps of Engineers
Eastman Lake
P.O. Box 67
Raymond, CA 93653
(209) 689-3255

Location

Eastman Lake, created by Buchanan Dam, lies in the foothills of the Sierra Nevada in central California on the Chowchilla River, approximately 25 miles northeast of the city of Chowchilla. Photographers will particularly enjoy the wildlife area, located at the north end of the lake.

Statistics

1,780 acres, surface area
5½ miles long
27 miles of shoreline

NOTE: Due to presence of hydrilla, lake is closed to boating; bank fishing is allowed only in designated area.

FACILITIES

RECREATION AREA	Camping — Developed sites	Camping — Undeveloped sites	Group Camping (Reservations Only)	Picnicking	Fishing Access	Boat Ramp	Swim Beach	Piped water	Restroom — flush	Restroom — portable	Hot water showers	Trailer dump station	Fish cleaning station	Campfire center	Information center	Hiking trail	Tot lot — playground	Hunting area	Telephone
CODORNIZ	●		●				●	●		●	●		●		●				●
CHOWCHILLA				●	●		●	●	●		●		●		●				
VISITOR CENTER					●		●							●	●				
WILDCAT	●				●			●							●				
MONUMENT RIDGE			●	●			●		●						●				
FISH AND WILDLIFE				●											●		●		
RAYMOND BRIDGE				●											●		●		

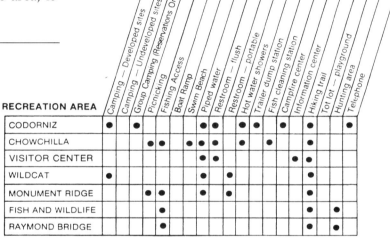

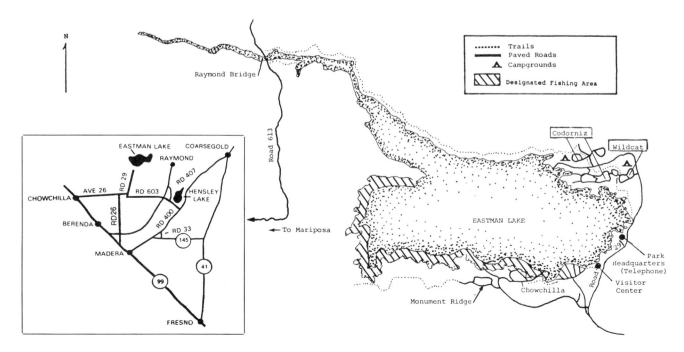

Legend:
```
........ Trails
———— Paved Roads
▲ Campgrounds
▨ Designated Fishing Area
```

Hensley Lake

For Information

Corps of Engineers
Hensley Lake
P.O. Box 85
Raymond, CA 93653
(209) 673-5151

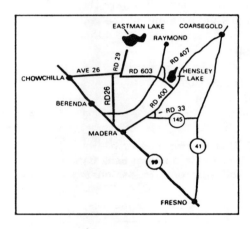

Location

Hensley Lake, formed by Hidden Dam, is on the Fresno River about 17 miles northeast of Madera. Located near the geographic center of California, the lake is situated in the oak woodland environment of the Sierra Nevada foothills.

Statistics

1,570 acres, surface area
3.2 miles long
24 miles of shoreline

FACILITIES

RECREATION AREA	Camping	Picnicking	Fishing Access	Launch Ramp	Swim Beach	Rest Rooms	Showers	Trailer Dump Station	Fish Cleaning Station	Campfire Center	Information Center	Telephone
Hidden View	●		●	●	●	●	●	●	●	●		●
Park Headquarters			●			●					●	●
Vista Point			●			●						
Buck Ridge		●	●	●	●	●			●			
Wakalumi	●		●			●						

Inyo National Forest

For Information

Forest Supervisor
Inyo National Forest
873 North Main Street
Bishop, CA 93514
(619) 873-2400

Location

The Inyo National Forest covers about 160 miles of the eastern Sierra Nevada Mountains as well as the Glass, the White, and portions of the Inyo Mountains. The forest lies east of Yosemite National Park, and reaches to the Nevada border in the eastern part of Central California. The national forest encompasses 1,905,939 acres.

Special Notes

The forest has Palisade Glacier, the southernmost glacier in the United States; Methuselah, the 4,600-year-old bristlecone pine; the Patriarch, the largest bristlecone pine; the largest Jeffrey pine forest in the world; and Mt. Whitney, the highest mountain in the contiguous United States. Access to a large portion of the Sequoia-Kings Canyon and Yosemite National Parks is through the west side of the Inyo National Forest. There are nearly 500 lakes and more than 100 streams that provide excellent fishing.

Winter sports are a major attraction at June Mountain and Mammoth Mountain ski areas. Backpackers and fishermen are replaced by skiers after the first good snows. Cross-country skiing has become a popular pastime also.

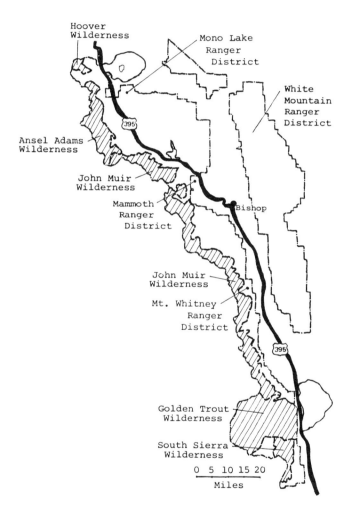

Wilderness Areas

Five Wilderness Areas are in the forest. The 63,000-acre *South Sierra Wilderness* straddles the Sierra Nevada crest at the southern end of the range. Elevations range from 6,100 feet near Kennedy Meadows to 12,123 feet at Olancha Peak. The wilderness also lies in the Sequoia National Forest and south side entry is made from that forest.

The *Golden Trout Wilderness*, also in the southern portion of the Inyo National Forest, encompasses 303,287 acres on Inyo and Sequoia National Forests. The western part is a large drainage basin surrounded by high, rugged mountains while the eastern part is an extension of the Kern Plateau.

Best travel is June through October; it is a good area for novice backpackers.

The *John Muir Wilderness*, the largest and most visited wilderness in the state, extends nearly 100 miles along the Sierra Nevada crest. This 584,000-acre wilderness has snow-capped mountains, hundreds of alpine lakes and streams, and elevations from 4,000 to more than 14,000 feet. The John Muir Trail and the Pacific Crest Trail traverse the area.

In 1984, the Minarets Wilderness was renamed the *Ansel Adams Wilderness*, in honor of the famous photographer and environmentalist. The 221,000 acres of rugged country includes the high country east of the Sierra crest with spectacular alpine scenery, and deep granite-walled gorges. This area is heavily used. Elevations range from 7,000 to 14,000 feet.

Approximately one-fifth of the 47,937 total acres in *Hoover Wilderness* is in Inyo National Forest; the larger portion is in Toiyabe National Forest. The area is extremely rugged with elevations from 8,000 to 14,000 feet, alpine lakes and meadows, and little timber. The best travel is July through September.

Mt. Whitney Ranger District

Campgrounds	Elevation (ft)	# of Units	Drinking Water	Toilets	Trailer Space	Fee Area
Horseshoe Meadow						
Golden Trout Backpacker	10,000	18	*	*		*
Cottonwood Lakes Backpacker	10,000	12	*	*		*
Horseshoe Meadow Equestrian	10,000	10	*	*	*	*
Roads End	9,400	15	str.	*	*	
Lone Pine Creek Drainage						
Lone Pine	6,000	43	*	*	*	*
Whitney Portal	8,000	44	*	F	*	*
Whitney Portal Group	8,000	(3)	*	F	*	*
Whitney Trailhead	8,300	10	*	F		*
Independence Creek Drainage						
Grays Meadow	6,000	52	*	F	*	*
Onion Valley	9,200	29	*	F		*
Oak Creek Drainage						
Oak Creek	5,000	24	*	*	*	*

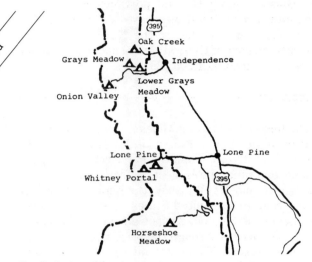

For Information

Mt. Whitney Ranger District
P.O. Box 8
Lone Pine, CA 93545
(619) 876-5542

Notes on Trailheads

Horseshoe Meadow is the trailhead to the Cottonwood Lakes Trail, which provides access to the southern portion of the John Muir Wilderness and Sequoia National Park, as well as access to the Golden Trout Wilderness.

Whitney Portal, along the *Lone Pine Creek Drainage*, is the trailhead to the 10.7-mile Mt. Whitney Trail, which leads to the highest peak in the "lower 48."

Onion Valley Campground, located along the *Independence Creek Drainage*, is the trailhead to the Kearsarge Pass Trail, which provides access to the spectacular backcountry of Kings Canyon National Park.

Notes:
Grays Meadow Campground and the 3 campgrounds at Whitney Portal are concessionaire operated; reservations are required for the 3 group camps through Mistix.

Use season is subject to weather conditions; Lone Pine and Oak Creek Campgrounds are open year-round; others vary from mid-May/July through mid-October/November.

4 campgrounds have a 1-day length of stay: Golden Trout Backpacker, Cottonwood Lakes Backpacker, Horseshoe Meadow Equestrian, and Whitney Trailhead.

Inyo National Forest *(continued)*

White Mountain Ranger District

Campgrounds	Elevation (ft)	# of Units	Drinking Water	Toilets	Trailer Space	Fee Area
Big Pine Creek Drainage						
Upper Sage Flat	7,600	21	*	*	*	*
Sage Flat	7,400	28	*	*	*	*
First Falls	8,300	5	str.	*		
Big Pine Creek	7,700	36	*	*	*	*
Palisade Group	7,600	(2)	*	F	*	*
Ancient Bristlecone Forest						
Grandview	8,600	26		*	*	
Pinon Group	7,200	(5)		*	*	*
Fossil Group	7,200	(11)		*	*	*
Poleta Group	7,200	(8)		*	*	*
Juniper Group	7,200	(5)		*	*	*
Bishop Creek Drainage						
Big Trees	7,500	9	*	F	*	*
Forks	7,800	9	*	F	*	*
Intake #2	7,500	20	*	*	*	*
Bishop Park Group	7,500	(1)	*	F	*	*
Bishop Park	7,500	20	*	F	*	*
Camp Sabrina	9,000	34	str.	*	*	
North Lake	9,500	11	*	F		*
Four Jeffrey	8,100	106	*	F	*	*
Mountain Glen	8,400	5	str.	*		
Aspen Meadow	8,500	5	str.	*		
Table Mountain	8,600	5	str.	*		
Willow	9,000	7	str.	*		

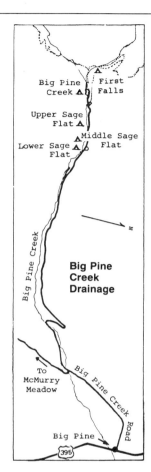

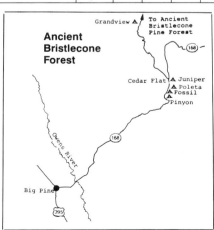

REGION 5

Inyo National Forest *(continued)*

White Mountain Ranger District (continued)

Campgrounds	Elevation (ft)	# of Units	Drinking Water	Toilets	Trailer Space	Fee Area
Rock Creek Drainage						
Tuff	7,000	34	*	F	*	*
French Camp	7,500	86	*	F	*	*
Holiday	7,500	33	*	*	*	*
Aspen Group	8,100	(5)	*	F		*
Iris Meadow	8,300	14	*	F	*	*
Big Meadow	8,600	11	*	F	*	*
Palisade	8,600	5	*	F	*	*
East Fork	9,000	133	*	F	*	*
Pine Grove	9,300	11	*	F	*	*
Rock Creek Lake	9,600	28	*	F	*	*
Rock Creek Lake Group	9,700	(10)	*	F		*
Mosquito Flat	10,000	19	*	F		*
Mosquito Flat Trailhead	10,000	10	str.	*		
Lower Rock Creek	6,500	5	str.	*	*	
McGee Creek Drainage						
McGee Creek	7,600	28	*	F	*	*
Upper McGee Creek	7,800	4	str.	*		

Notes:

McGee Creek and the 5 campgrounds in Big Pine Creek Drainage are concessionaire operated.

Advance reservations are required for all group campgrounds through Mistix.

Use season is subject to weather conditions; normal use season is April/May through September/November.

The 4 group campgrounds in Ancient Bristlecone Forest are open year-round.

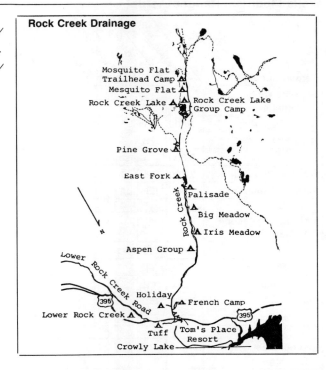

Rock Creek Drainage

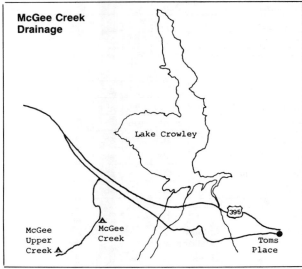

McGee Creek Drainage

For Information

White Mountain Ranger District
798 North Main Street
Bishop, CA 93514
(619) 873-2500

The bristlecone pines of the Ancient Bristlecone Forest (page 57) are said to be the world's oldest living things.

Inyo National Forest *(continued)*

Mammoth Ranger District

Campgrounds	Elevation (ft)	# of Units	Drinking Water	Toilets	Trailer Space	Fee Area
Convict Creek Drainage						
Convict Lake	7,600	88	*	F	*	*
Mammoth Village Area						
New Shady Rest	7,800	97	*	F	*	*
Old Shady Rest	7,800	51	*	F	*	*
Sherwin Creek	7,600	87	*	*	*	*
Pine Glen Group	7,800	(12)	*	F	*	*
Pine Glen	7,800	7	*	F	*	*
Mammoth Lakes Basin						
Twin Lakes	8,900	97	*	F	*	*
Lake Mary	8,900	51	*	F	*	*
Pine City	8,900	11	*	F		*
Coldwater	8,900	79	*	F	*	*
Lake George	9,000	22	*	F	*	*
Horseshoe Lake Group	8,900	(8)	*	F	*	*

Campgrounds	Elevation (ft)	# of Units	Drinking Water	Toilets	Trailer Space	Fee Area
Reds Meadow Drainage						
Agnew Meadows	8,400	24	*	F	*	*
Agnew Meadows Group	8,400	(4)	*	F	*	*
Soda Springs	7,700	29	*	F	*	*
Pumice Flat	7,700	17	*	F	*	*
Pumice Flat Group	7,700	(4)	*	F	*	*
Minaret Falls	7,600	27	*	F	*	*
Reds Meadow	7,600	74	*	F	*	*

Notes:

Advance reservations are required for the group campgrounds through Mistix.

Use season is subject to weather conditions; campgrounds are open May/June through September/October.

Sherwin Creek is concessionaire operated.

For Information

Mammoth Ranger District
P.O. Box 148
Mammoth Lakes, CA 93546
(619) 924-5500

A shuttle bus service operates during the hours of 10 am and 5 pm to transport passengers to various locations between Agnew Meadows and Reds Meadow in the Devils Postpile National Monument area. Day users and backpackers entering the valley when the shuttle is operating must ride the bus. The charge is one dollar per person.

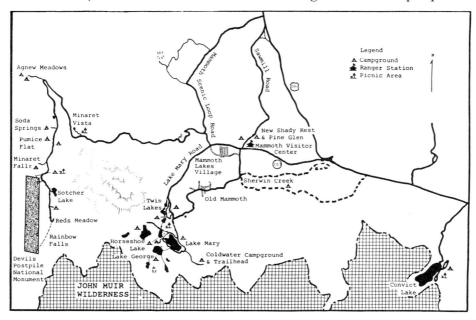

Inyo National Forest *(continued)*

Mono Lake Ranger District

Campgrounds	Elevation (ft)	# of Units	Drinking Water	Toilets	Trailer Space	Fee Area
Crestview Area						
Glass Creek	7,600	30	str.	P	*	
Big Springs	7,300	24	str.	P	*	
Deadman	7,800	30	str.	P	*	
Hartley Springs	8,400	21		P	*	
June Lake Loop						
Oh! Ridge	7,600	148	*	F	*	*
June Lake	7,600	22	*	F	*	*
Gull Lake	7,600	12	*	F	*	*
Reversed Creek	7,600	17	*	F	*	*
Silver Lake	7,200	65	*	F	*	*
Aerie Crag	7,300	20	*	F		*
Lee Vining Creek Drainage						
Big Bend	7,800	18	*	V	*	*
Ellery Lake	9,500	13	*	V	*	*
Junction	9,600	10	str.	V	*	
Tioga Lake	9,700	13	*	V		*
Sawmill	9,800	9	str.	V		
Saddlebag Lake	10,000	22	*	V		*

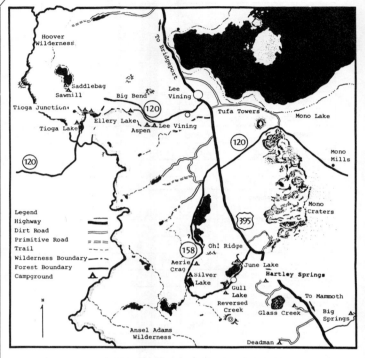

Notes:

Oh! Ridge and June Lake Campgrounds are concessionaire operated.

Lee Vining and Aspen Grove Campgrounds in the Lee Vining area (see map) are operated by Mono County.

Use season is subject to weather conditions; normal season is May/June through October.

For Information

Mono Lake Ranger District
P.O. Box 429
Lee Vining, CA 93541
(619) 647-6525

Mono Lake's tufa towers were formed by the interaction of springs with lake water, and are now exposed by a 40-ft drop in water level during the last 40 years.

Isabella Lake

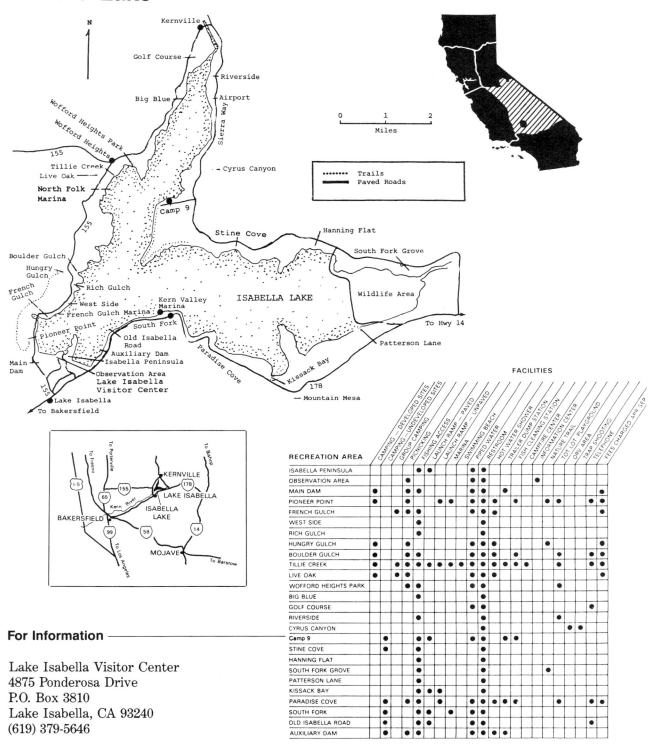

RECREATION AREA	CAMPING — DEVELOPED SITES	CAMPING — UNDEVELOPED SITES	GROUP CAMPING	PICNICKING	FISHING ACCESS	LAUNCH RAMP — PAVED	LAUNCH RAMP — UNPAVED	MARINA	SWIMMING BEACH	PIPED WATER	RESTROOM	HOT WATER SHOWER	TRAILER DUMP STATION	FISH CLEANING STATION	CAMPFIRE CENTER	INFORMATION CENTER	NATURE TRAIL	TOT LOT PLAYGROUND	ORV AREA	TRAP SHOOTING	TELEPHONE	FEES CHARGED APR–SEP
ISABELLA PENINSULA				●	●					●	●											
OBSERVATION AREA			●							●	●					●						
MAIN DAM	●			●	●					●	●		●									●
PIONEER POINT	●			●		●	●	●		●	●	●		●			●	●			●	●
FRENCH GULCH			●	●	●					●	●	●										
WEST SIDE				●							●											
RICH GULCH				●							●											
HUNGRY GULCH	●			●						●	●	●					●					●
BOULDER GULCH	●			●						●	●	●	●					●			●	●
TILLIE CREEK	●		●	●	●	●	●	●	●	●	●	●	●	●			●			●	●
LIVE OAK	●		●	●						●	●	●										●
WOFFORD HEIGHTS PARK			●	●						●	●						●					
BIG BLUE				●							●											
GOLF COURSE				●						●	●									●		
RIVERSIDE				●							●						●	●				
CYRUS CANYON											●								●	●		
Camp 9	●			●	●					●	●		●	●								
STINE COVE	●			●							●											
HANNING FLAT				●							●											
SOUTH FORK GROVE				●							●					●						
PATTERSON LANE				●							●											
KISSACK BAY				●	●	●					●											
PARADISE COVE		●		●	●		●			●	●	●	●	●			●			●	●	
SOUTH FORK		●		●	●		●			●	●											
OLD ISABELLA ROAD		●		●	●					●	●										●	
AUXILIARY DAM		●		●	●					●	●	●	●									

For Information

Lake Isabella Visitor Center
4875 Ponderosa Drive
P.O. Box 3810
Lake Isabella, CA 93240
(619) 379-5646

Location

Isabella Lake, located on the Kern River, 45 miles northeast of Bakersfield, offers a broad expanse of clear, cool water in a semi-arid environment.

Statistics

11,200 acres, surface area
8.5 miles long
38 miles of shoreline

Kings Canyon National Park

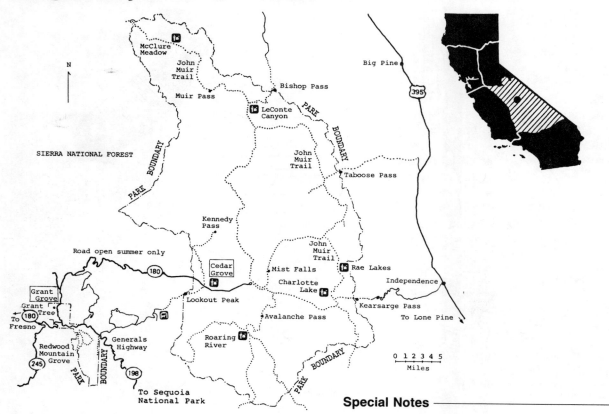

SEQUOIA NATIONAL FOREST

For Information

Superintendent
Sequoia and Kings Canyon National Parks
Three Rivers, CA 93271
(209) 565-3456

Location

Kings Canyon National Park is reached by proceeding east on SH 180 from U.S. 99 at Fresno, or from the south via the Generals Highway from Sequoia National Park. The Grant Grove area (elevation 6,500 feet), a detached section of the park, is the most developed portion. The Cedar Grove area (elevation 4,630 feet) is located 32 miles east of Grant Grove on SH 180 and serves as a popular base for extensive trail trips into the surrounding high country. The 461,636-acre park has more than 456,000 acres designated as wilderness.

Special Notes

The top attraction in the General Grant Grove, located a mile west of Grant Grove Village, is the General Grant Tree, second-largest living thing in the world. The Grant Tree is nearly as tall as the General Sherman Tree, and actually has a slightly larger base diameter. The General Grant Tree has been designated "The Nation's Christmas Tree," and a special ceremony is held each December.

At Grant Grove Village, a narrow paved road branches northeast from SR 180 and climbs 2.6 miles to Panoramic Point. From this overlook, much of the Kings Canyon country is visible; the deep canyons of the Middle and South Forks of the Kings River, portions of the Sierra Nevada crest and the northern end of the Great Western Divide. John Muir found the Valley of the Kings, one of the deepest gorges in North America, even "grander" than Yosemite Valley.

Kings Canyon National Park adjoins Sequoia National Park to the south; these adjoining parks are part of the enormous area of public land that occupies most of the Sierra Nevada. They are almost completely surrounded by national forests. There are more than 800 miles of trails and 1,000 glacial lakes nestled at elevations higher than 10,000 feet in the two parks.

Kings Canyon National Park *(continued)*

Warm daytime and cool evening temperatures characterize summer in Grant Grove. Occasional afternoon thundershowers can be expected. A deep blanket of snow often covers this area from December to May. Cedar Grove is closed in the winter due to hazardous road conditions, but summer temperatures are generally hot, at times reaching the high 90s. However, a constant breeze makes it quite pleasant. For the backpackers in the High Sierras, summer weather is remarkably pleasant by mountain standards, but there are wide swings in daytime temperatures. Night temperatures in the summer often drop into the low 30s, occasionally dipping into the 20s.

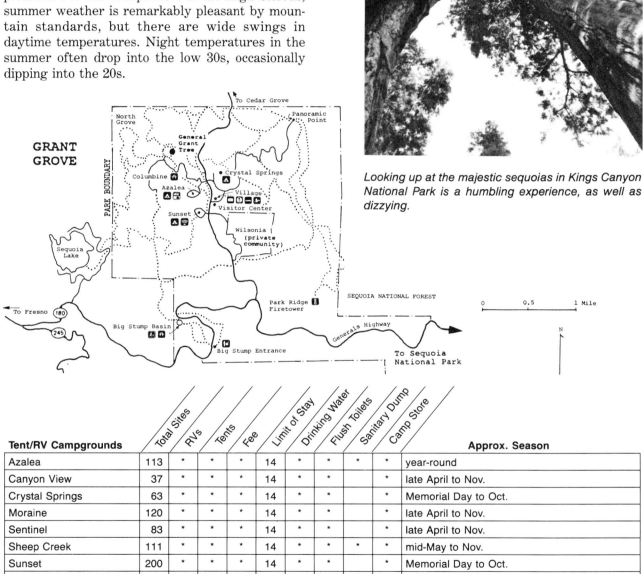

Looking up at the majestic sequoias in Kings Canyon National Park is a humbling experience, as well as dizzying.

Tent/RV Campgrounds	Total Sites	RVs	Tents	Fee	Limit of Stay	Drinking Water	Flush Toilets	Sanitary Dump	Camp Store	Approx. Season
Azalea	113	*	*	*	14	*	*	*	*	year-round
Canyon View	37	*	*	*	14	*	*		*	late April to Nov.
Crystal Springs	63	*	*	*	14	*	*		*	Memorial Day to Oct.
Moraine	120	*	*	*	14	*	*		*	late April to Nov.
Sentinel	83	*	*	*	14	*	*		*	late April to Nov.
Sheep Creek	111	*	*	*	14	*	*	*	*	mid-May to Nov.
Sunset	200	*	*	*	14	*	*		*	Memorial Day to Oct.
Group Campground										
Canyon View	4	*	*	*	14	*	*		*	late April to Nov.
Backcountry Campsites										
Various locations (hike-in, horseback ride-in)	ltd		*							

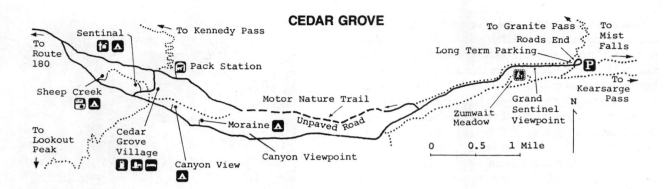

CEDAR GROVE

Facilities & Activities

park entrance fee

camping permitted only in designated campgrounds or in backcountry areas

3 campgrounds (see chart and map) with 376 campsites at Grant Grove; no reservations; Azalea Campground open all year, others open approx. late April—Nov.

4 campgrounds (see chart and map) with 351 campsites at Cedar Grove; no reservations; open approx. late April—Nov.

Canyon View Group Campground (see chart) at Cedar Grove; 4 sites, each with 20 min./60 max. persons; summers only; reservations required

limit of stay between June 14–Sept. 14 is 14 days; limit of stay between Sept. 15–June 13 is 30 days

Azalea and Sentinel Campgrounds have handicapped-accessible campsites

sanitary dump stations at Canyon View and Sheep Creek Campgrounds are open only May—October

backcountry camping (June—Nov. recommended): permit required; reservations accepted beginning March 1; half of permits available on a first-come, first-served basis

fires permitted only in designated fire rings

picnicking

bicycling/rentals at Cedar Grove

no motorcycles or bicycles allowed on trails; may be used only on roadways

horseback riding: day trips from Grant Grove; at pack station in Cedar Grove

fishing

hiking trails (over 800 miles in Kings Canyon and Sequoia combined)

self-guiding interpretive trails/exhibits

General Grant Tree Trail

snow-shoe hiking/cross-country skiing at snow play area at Big Stump and Azalea Campground (Dec.—April)

motor tours

visitor center at Grant Grove

ranger-guided nature walks/evening ranger programs at Grant Grove and Cedar Grove

lodging, food service, supplies, service station, showers, at Cedar Grove Village and Grant Grove Village

pets must be on leash; not allowed on any park trails

the *Sequoia Bark*, the park's free newspaper, has current information on services and activities; available at visitor center and entrance stations

Grant Grove is home to the second largest living thing in the world—a sequoia named General Grant (see page 79).

Lake Kaweah

For Information

Corps of Engineers
Lake Kaweah
P.O. Box 346
Lemoncove, CA 93244
(209) 597-2301

Location

Lake Kaweah was formed by Terminus Dam, constructed on the Kaweah River about 20 miles east of Visalia. The lake is in the foothills of the Sierra Nevada, at the gateway to Sequoia-Kings Canyon National Park. There is a substantial drop in lake level each summer.

Statistics

1,913 acres, surface area
5 miles long
22 miles of shoreline

RECREATION AREA	CAMPING – DEVELOPED SITES	CAMPING – UNDEVELOPED SITES	GROUP CAMPING – UNDEVELOPED SITES	PICNICKING	FISHING ACCESS	LAUNCH RAMP	MARINA	PIPED WATER	RESTROOM – FLUSH	RESTROOM – PORTABLE	SHOWERS – HOT	TRAILER DUMP STATION	FISH CLEANING STATION	CAMPFIRE CENTER	INFORMATION CENTER	NATURE TRAIL	TOT LOT – PLAYGROUND
OBSERVATION														●			
LEMON HILL				●	●	●			●								
KAWEAH			●	●	●		●	●	●	●				●			
HORSE CREEK	●	●		●			●	●	●	●	●	●	●	●	●	●	●
SLICK ROCK			●	●					●								
LIME KILN		●							●								

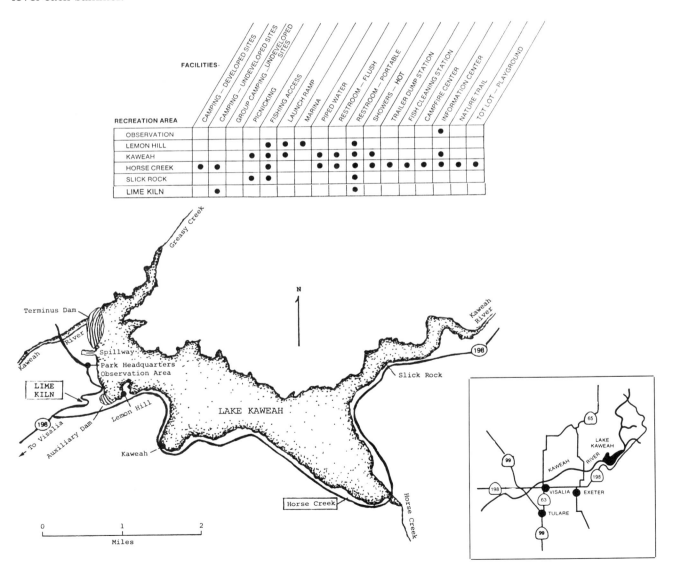

McConnell State Recreation Area

For Information

McConnell State Recreation Area
McConnell Road
Ballico, CA 95303
(209) 394-7755

Location

McConnell State Recreation Area is located 5 miles southeast of Delhi, 11 miles southeast of Turlock, and 25 miles northwest of Merced. To reach it from Highway 99, turn east on El Capitan at Delhi and drive to Pepper Road; turn right and follow the signs. The 74-acre park, with a 104-foot elevation, is in Merced County.

Facilities & Activities

17 developed campsites
showers
24-foot trailers; 27-foot campers/motorhomes
group camping area (110 max.)
picnicking
group picnicking area (150 max.)
fishing
swimming
on State Park Reservation System
    (mid-May—mid-Sept.)

Special Notes

Located in the San Joaquin Valley, this recreation area offers year-round recreation in a shady oasis, a small island of peace and quiet in the midst of twenty million Californians. The low, easy, summer flow of the Merced River is great for swimming.

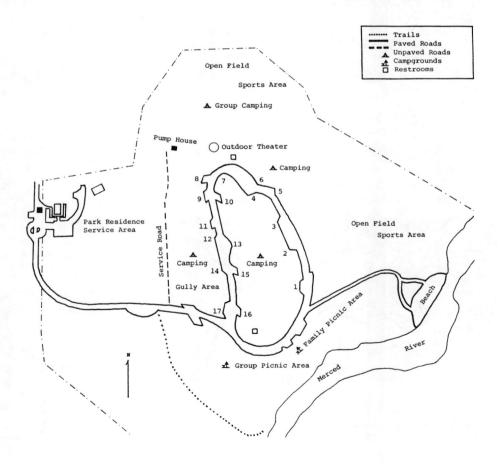

Millerton Lake State Recreation Area

For Information

Millerton Lake State Recreation Area
P.O. Box 205
Friant, CA 93626
(209) 822-2332

Location

Millerton Lake State Recreation Area is located in Fresno and Madera Counties at an elevation of 600 feet and encompasses 6,553 acres. The park headquarters is 20 miles northeast of Fresno via SH 41 and Friant Road. The campground on the north shore is 20 miles east of Madera via SH 145 and North Fork Road.

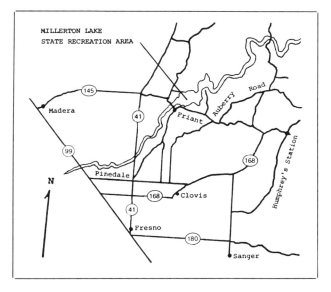

Facilities & Activities

3 improved campgrounds
133 developed campsites
outdoor cold showers
31-foot trailers; 31-foot campers/motorhomes
trailer sanitation station
2 group camps—on State Park Reservation
　System (mid-March—mid-Sept.)
　Large Group Camp (75 persons/25 vehicle max.)
　Small Group Camp (40 person/15 vehicle max.)
　　(developed sites; outdoor cold showers; 31-foot
　　trailer max.; bus parking; can be reserved
　　together for group up to 115)
picnicking
fishing
hiking trail
swimming
exhibits
horseback riding trail
boating (launch ramp; mooring; rentals; water
　skiing; on-board camping; boat-in-camping at
　Temperance Flat Boat Camp, 25 sites)
on State Park Reservation System
　(mid-March—mid-Sept.)

Home sweet home—for a few days anyway.

Special Notes

Millerton Lake, formed by the Friant Dam across the San Joaquin River, has 43 miles of shoreline for water sports. The surrounding hills offer good hiking and a surprising variety of wildlife can be observed. A mile wide near the damsite, Millerton Lake is 3 miles wide at its widest point and stretches more than 16 miles back up into the river canyon. The park also contains the original Millerton County Courthouse, built in 1867.

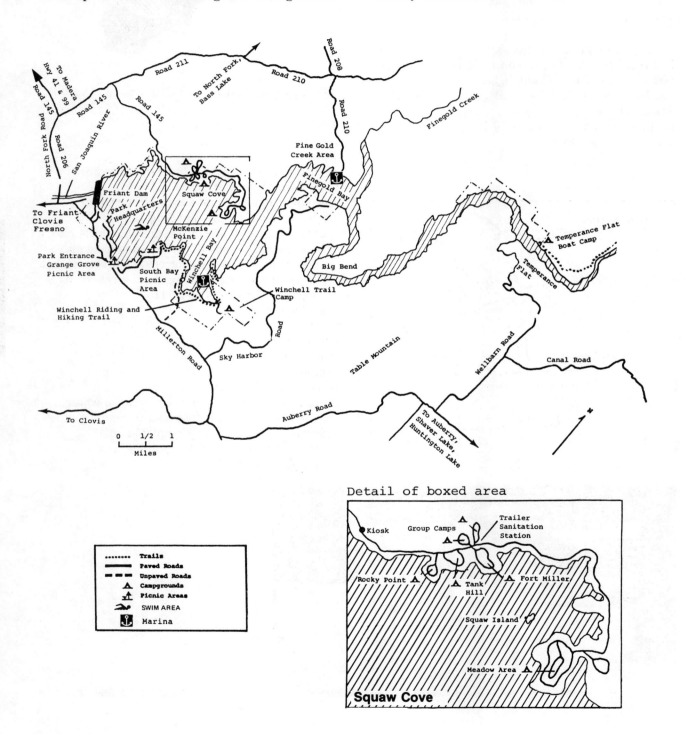

Detail of boxed area

Squaw Cove

Mountain Home State Forest

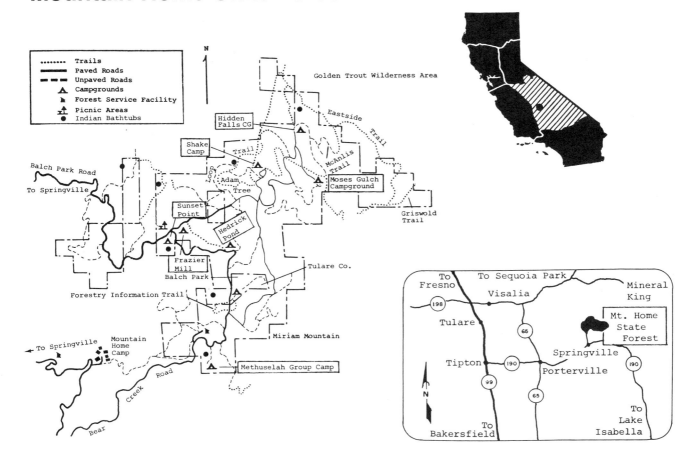

For Information

Mountain Home State Forest
P.O. Box 517
Springville, CA 93265
(209) 539-2855 (winter)
(209) 539-2321 (summer)

Location

Mountain Home State Forest is located northeast of Porterville off of SH 190 and north of Springville on J37. The 4,809-acre state forest is within the Sequoia National Forest on the boundary of the Golden Trout Wilderness. Elevation ranges from 5,100–7,600 feet.

Facilities & Activities

7 campgrounds; 96 rustic campsites; no fee; no permit necessary to build fires in camp stoves provided

no open fires
80 rustic campsites at Balch Park, operated by Tulare County; fee charged
camping season from May—Nov. (or as snow conditions allow)
camp only in improved campsites
3 ponds stocked with catchable rainbow trout
fishing in the North Fork of the Middle Fork of the Tule River and its tributary streams
hunting in season
numerous hiking trails and horseback trails
guide service and rental horses available at Pack Station located near Shake Camp
picnic site at Old Mountain Home

Special Notes

Adam Tree, on the Loop Trail that begins and ends at Shake Camp, is one of the largest trees in the forest; 27 feet in diameter at base and 240 feet tall.

"Indian bathtubs," also on the Loop Trail plus other sites, are curious deep basins formed in solid granite used by the ancient people of the area.

Pine Flat Lake

For Information

Corps of Engineers
Pine Flat Lake
P.O. Box 117
Piedra, CA 93649
(209) 787-2589

Location

Pine Flat Lake is on the Kings River about 32 miles east of Fresno, in the oak-covered foothills of the Sierra Nevada. Water levels fluctuate daily.

Statistics

6,000 acres, surface area
21 miles long
67 miles of shoreline

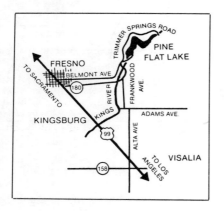

RECREATION AREA	CAMPING	GROUP CAMPING	PICNICKING	OVERNIGHT MOORING	FISHING ACCESS	LAUNCH RAMP	MARINA	PIPED WATER	REST ROOM	HOT WATER SHOWER	R.V. SANITARY DUMP	FISH CLEANING STATION	CAMPFIRE CENTER	NATURE TRAIL	TELEPHONE	FEES CHARGED APR.-SEPT.	OPERATED BY
OBSERVATION AREA			•		•				•								CORPS OF ENGINEERS
DEER CREEK			•	•	•	•			•								CORPS OF ENGINEERS
ISLAND PARK	•		•		•	•	•	•	•	•	•	•	•	•	•	•	CORPS OF ENGINEERS
DEER CREEK POINT		•						•	•							•	CORPS OF ENGINEERS
LAKEVIEW					•	•			•								CORPS OF ENGINEERS
TRIMMER	•		•		•	•		•	•						•	•	CORPS OF ENGINEERS
CHOINUMNI	•		•		•			•	•		•						FRESNO COUNTY
PINE FLAT	•	•	•		•			•	•		•					•	FRESNO COUNTY
SYCAMORE	•	•	•						•								CORPS OF ENGINEERS
LAKEVIEW			•						•								CORPS OF ENGINEERS
KIRCH FLAT	•		•						•								FOREST SERVICE
ZEBE CREEK			•	•	•				•								CORPS OF ENGINEERS
LAWLESS COVE			•	•	•				•								CORPS OF ENGINEERS
FLUME COVE			•	•	•				•								CORPS OF ENGINEERS
EDISON POINT			•	•					•								CORPS OF ENGINEERS
SWINGING BRIDGE COVE			•	•	•				•								CORPS OF ENGINEERS
HORSE COLLAR			•	•	•				•								CORPS OF ENGINEERS

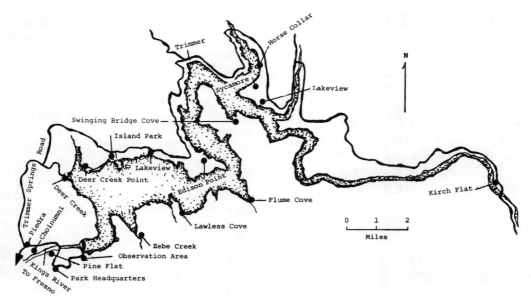

Red Rock Canyon State Park

For Information

Red Rock Canyon State Park
RRC, Box 26
Cantil, CA 93519
(805) 942-0662

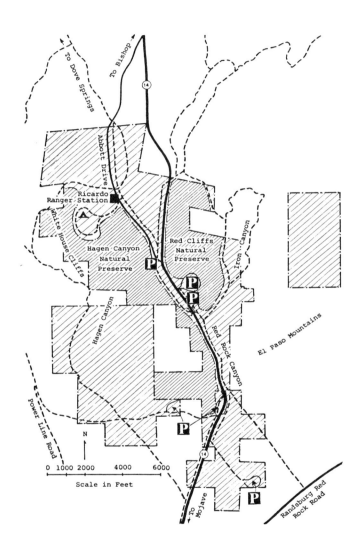

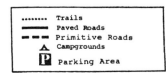

Trails ....
Paved Roads ——————
Primitive Roads — — —
Campgrounds ▲
Parking Area 🄿

Location

Red Rock Canyon State Park, with its scenic desert cliffs, buttes, and spectacular rock formations, is located 25 miles northeast of Mojave on Highway 14. With an elevation of 2,600 feet, the 3,984-acre park is located in Kern County.

Facilities & Activities

50 primitive campsites
campsites for disabled
no showers
30-foot trailers; 30-foot campers/motorhomes
trailer sanitation station
picnicking
hiking trails
nature trails
exhibits
vehicular recreation opportunities on designated primitive dirt roads (MC, 4WD, ATV, DB)

Special Notes

Spring is the most popular season at Red Rock Canyon, but the area remains open year-round. Summer can be very hot during the day. Winter is quite cool with night temperatures often dipping well below freezing. This park was made for camera buffs as each tributary canyon is unique, with colors ranging dramatically from stark white to vivid reds and dark chocolate browns. After a wet winter the floral displays are stunning.

Off-highway vehicles are permitted in the campground and may also use the primitive roads designated for travel. Only foot travel is permitted within the natural preserves.

REGION 5

Sequoia National Forest

For Information

Forest Supervisor
Sequoia National Forest
900 West Grand Avenue
Porterville, CA 93257
(209) 784-1500

Location

Sequoia National Forest, located at the southern end of the Sierra Nevada Mountains in central California, extends from the Kings River on the north to the Kern River and Piute Mountain Range on the south. The eastern boundary is on the Sierra Nevada summit where it joins the Inyo National Forest. The 1,180,042-acre Forest extends west to the brush-covered foothills along the San Joaquin Valley.

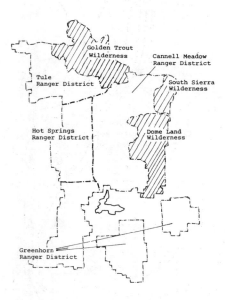

Special Notes

The Sequoia National Forest contains 30 groves of the giant Sequoia. These groves vary from a hundred trees or less to groves containing thousands of awe-inspiring specimens. The Boole Tree, the world's largest in circumference, stands 269 feet high, has a circumference of 112 feet, and a base diameter of 35 feet. This giant sequoia is located just north of Converse Mountain, 3/4-mile from the end of the dirt road in Converse Basin in the Hume Lake Ranger District.

The immensity of a sequoia is best experienced when you drive "through" one.

Sequoia National Forest (continued)

Elevations on the forest range from 1,000 to 12,000 feet. Precipitous canyons and mountain streams form spectacular waterfalls such as South Creek Falls near Johnsondale and Grizzly Falls near Cedar Grove. Dome Rock is one of several opportunities for the photographer along the Western Divide Highway (SH 190 just south of Peppermint Campground). This massive granite monolith forms a natural vista point overlooking the Kern River Canyon.

Winter activities include downhill skiing at Shirley Meadow on weekends and holidays in December through March, if snow is sufficient. Cross-country skiing and snowmobiling are popular activities in snowplay areas such as Cherry Gap and Quail Flat on the Hume Lake Ranger District, and in the vicinity of Quaking Aspen Campground on the Tule River Ranger District.

Commercial whitewater raft trips are available on the Kern River—a river unique among California's great rivers, as it flows north-south instead of east-west for 100 of its 165 miles. With a gradient exceeding 30 feet per mile, the Kern is one of the steeper and wilder whitewater runs in the state. Commercial raft trips are also available on Kings River beginning above Mill Flat Campground in the Hume Lake Ranger District.

Wilderness Areas

Mountains of the South Sierra offer diverse opportunities for recreation experiences in five wildernesses. *Monarch Wilderness* offers rugged, rocky, steep, and inaccessible canyons north and south of the Kings River. Extremely scenic, Monarch encompasses 56,952 acres on Sequoia and Sierra National Forests and has elevations ranging from 2,300 feet to 11,077 feet at Hogback Peak.

The 10,500-acre *Jennie Lakes Wilderness* includes Jennie and Weaver Lakes, several smaller lakes, many rock outcrops, and three mountain peaks. It is adjacent to the western boundary of Sequoia and Kings Canyon National Parks. Elevations range from 6,800 to 10,365 feet at the summit of Mitchell Peak.

Golden Trout Wilderness encompasses 303,287 acres on Sequoia and Inyo National Forests. The western part is a large drainage basin surrounded by high, rugged mountains; the eastern part is an extension of the Kern Plateau. Its many lush meadows and vast conifer forests spring from granitic geology. It is a good area for novice backpackers.

Fragile meadowlands, diversity of flora and fauna between forested ridges, rolling hills, and craggy, steep peaks describe the *South Sierra Wilderness*. A relatively gentle terrain area of 24,650 acres on the Sequoia National Forest portion is ideally suited to family-oriented recreation. The more adventurous can frequent the 38,350 acres along the Sierra Crest on the Inyo Forest, which completes the new 63,000-acre South Sierra Wilderness. Elevations range from 6,100 feet near Kennedy Meadows to the summit of Olancha Peak at 12,123 feet.

Dome Land Wilderness, with a total acreage of 94,696, is known for its many granite domes and unique geologic formations. The semi-arid to arid country has elevations ranging from 3,000 to 9,730 feet. Some areas of the Wilderness are extremely rugged while others have a more gentle terrain.

The wilderness areas of our national forests provide unique outdoor adventures for experienced mountaineers and family campers.

Hume Lake Ranger District

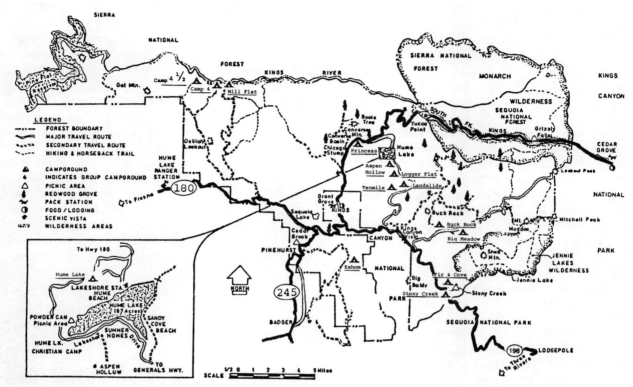

For Information

Hume Lake Ranger District
35860 East Kings Canyon Road
Dunlap, CA 93621
(209) 338-2251

Campgrounds	Elevation (ft)	# of Units	Drinking Water	Toilets	Trailer Space	Fee Area
Big Meadow	7,600	25		*	*	
Buck Rock	7,600	5		*	*	
Camp 4	1,000	5		*		
Camp 4½	1,000	5		*		
Eshom	4,800	17		*	*	
Hume Lake	5,200	75	*	*	*	*
Landslide	5,800	6		*		
Mill Flat	1,000	5		*		
Princess	5,900	90	*	*	*	*
Stony Creek	6,400	49	*	*	*	*
Tenmile	5,800	5		*		
Group Campgrounds						
Aspen Hollow	5,300	75	*	*	*	*
Cove	6,500	50	*	*		*
Fir	6,500	100	*	*		*
Logger Flat	5,300	50	*	*		*

Note: Reservations required for all group campgrounds through
Mistix.

Sequoia National Forest *(continued)*

Tule Ranger District

Campgrounds	Elevation (ft)	# of Units	Drinking Water	Toilets	Trailer Space	Fee Area
Belknap	4,800	15	*	*		*
Coffee Camp	2,000	18	*	*		*
Coy Flat	5,000	20	*	*	*	*
Peppermint	7,100	19		*		
Quaking Aspen	7,000	32	*	*	*	*
Wishon	4,000	35	*	*	*	*
Group Campground						
Quaking Aspen	7,000	4	*	*		*

Note:

All campgrounds are open May through October.

Quaking Aspen Group Campground (2 sites for 25 persons each; 2 sites for 50 persons each) requires advance registration through the ranger district office.

For Information

Tule Ranger District
32588 Highway 190
Springville, CA 93265
(209) 539-2607

Cross country and downhill skiing are popular at many state and national parks.

REGION 5

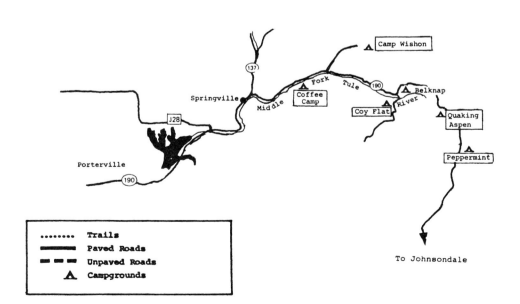

Legend:
.... **Trails**
——— **Paved Roads**
— — — **Unpaved Roads**
▲ **Campgrounds**

Sequoia National Forest *(continued)*

Hot Springs Ranger District

Campgrounds	Elevation (ft)	# of Units	Drinking Water	Toilets	Trailer Space	Fee Area
Deer Creek Mill	5,080	6	*	*		
Frog Meadow	7,500	10		*		
Holey Meadow	6,400	10	*	*	*	*
Leavis Flat	3,100	9	*	*	*	*
Long Meadow	6,000	6		*		
Lower Peppermint	5,300	17	*	*		*
Panorama	6,800	10		*		
Redwood Meadow	6,500	15	*	*		*
White River	4,000	12	*	*	*	*

Note:
Leavis Flat Campground is open year-long; all others are open from May or June until October 15.

For Information

Hot Springs Ranger District
Route 4, Box 548
California Hot Springs, CA 93207
(805) 548-6503

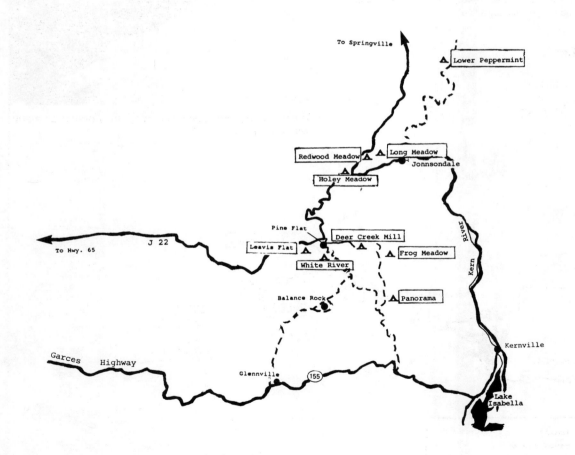

Sequoia National Forest (*continued*)

Cannell Meadow Ranger District

Campgrounds	Elevation (ft)	# of Units	Drinking Water	Toilets	Trailer Space	Fee Area
Camp 3	2,800	52	*	*	27' max	*
Fair View	3,500	55	*	*	*	*
Fish Creek	7,400	40	*	*	*	
Goldledge	3,200	37	*	*	*	*
Headquarters	2,700	44	*	*	*	*
Horse Meadow	7,600	41	*	*	*	
Hospital Flat	2,900	40	*	*	*	*
Kennedy Meadows	5,800	38	*	*	*	
Limestone	3,800	22		*	*	
Troy Meadows	7,800	73	*	*	*	

Note:
Headquarters Campground is open year-round; the rest are open May through November.

For Information

Cannell Meadow Ranger District
105 Whitney Road
P.O. Box 6
Kernville, CA 93238
(619) 376-3781

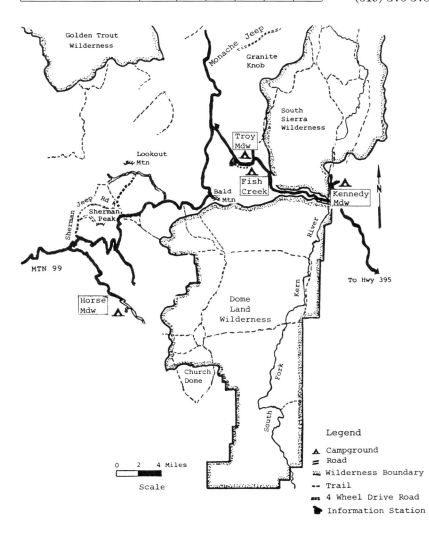

Legend

△ Campground
⇔ Road
𝚼 Wilderness Boundary
-- Trail
🚙 4 Wheel Drive Road
⬤ Information Station

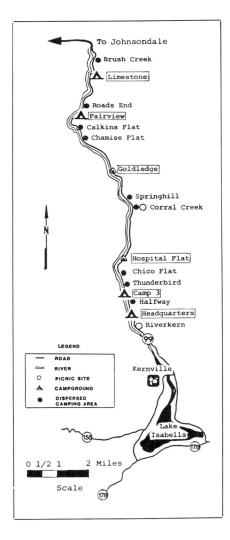

Sequoia National Forest *(continued)*

Greenhorn Ranger District

Campground	Elevation (ft)	# of Units	Drinking Water	Toilets	Trailer Space	Fee Area
Alder Creek	3,900	12		*	20 ft max.	
Breckenridge	7,100	8		*		
Cedar Creek	4,800	10	*	*		
Evans Flat	6,200	16		*	20 ft max.	
Hobo	2,300	35	*	*		*

Note:
Cedar Creek is open all year; the others are open May through September or October.

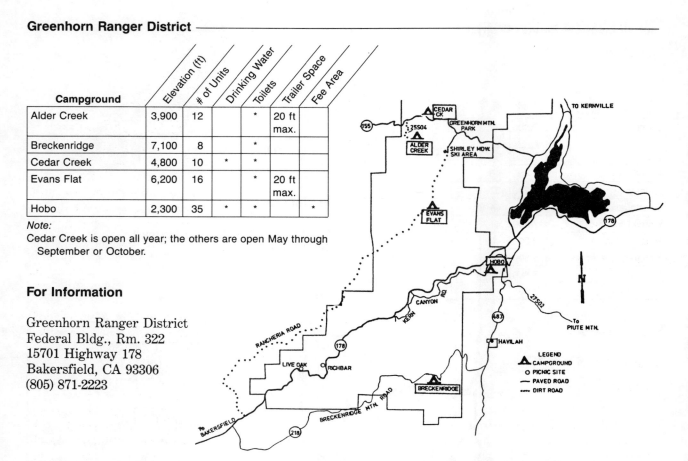

For Information

Greenhorn Ranger District
Federal Bldg., Rm. 322
15701 Highway 178
Bakersfield, CA 93306
(805) 871-2223

When learning to ski, it's important to remember which skis are yours.

Sequoia National Park

For Information

Superintendent
Sequoia and Kings Canyon National Parks
Three Rivers, CA 93271
(209) 565-3456

Location

Sequoia National Park is reached from the south via SH 198 from U.S. 99. The Generals Highway passes through Sequoia National Park to the Grant Grove area in Kings Canyon National Park and connects to SH 180. No roads cross the east-west width of the parks. The section of the Generals Highway from this southern park entrance to Giant Forest is extremely narrow and climbs 5,000 feet in 17 miles. Trailers 16 feet or longer are advised to use SH 180, through Kings Canyon National Park, for an easier, straighter road. The 402,487-acre park has more than 280,000 acres designated as wilderness.

Special Notes

The Generals Highway winds through the sequoia belt for a pleasant 2-hour drive of 46 miles from the Ash Mountain Entrance (in Sequoia National Park), to Grant Grove (in Kings Canyon National Park). Several branch roads take you to other scenic attractions. The Generals Highway between Lodgepole and Grant Grove is open year-round, but may be closed during winter months for several days at a time due to heavy snow. Great groves of giant sequoias, Mineral King Valley, and 14,495-foot

Mount Whitney, the highest mountain in the contiguous 48 states, are spectacular attractions here in the High Sierra.

The Mineral King area lies 25 miles southeast of Three Rivers at the end of a winding road. This road is closed from about November 1 to May 30. The beauty of its open sub-alpine meadows and towering timberline peaks is best seen by hiking to one of the lake basins that surround the 7,500-foot valley floor. All trails climb steeply from the valley floor. Facilities are rustic and limited.

Within the Giant Forest, a forested plateau, grow the largest living things on the face of this planet—the giant sequoias. Although these trees grow naturally in 75 separate locations along the western slope of the Sierra Nevada, four of the five largest sequoia specimens stand within the Giant Forest. The General Sherman remains recognized as the world's largest living thing, estimated at about 2,500 years.

Other attractions include Crescent Meadow, Crystal Cave, Tokopah Valley and Falls, and impressive Moro Rock, a granite monolith that juts

REGION 5

The largest living thing in the world—the sequoia named General Sherman—is more than 2,500 years old, 275 ft tall, and 36½ ft in diameter.

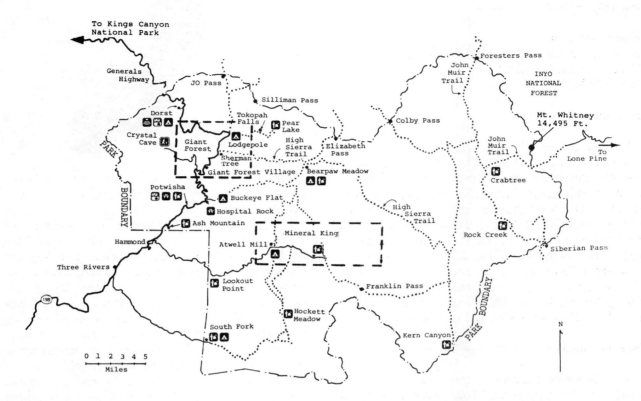

upward from the edge of the Giant Forest plateau and overlooks the deep canyon of the Kaweah River's middle fork. Steep granite steps climb 300 vertical feet to the 6,725-foot summit, where one of the best views in the southern Sierra Nevada awaits the visitor. To the east is the Great Western Divide, a series of serrated summits.

Facilities & Activities

park entrance fee

camping permitted only in designated campgrounds or in backcountry areas

Lodgepole Campground at Giant Forest, with 260 campsites; reservations through Ticketron, Memorial Day—Labor Day; first-come, first-served at other times; open all year

4 campgrounds (see chart and map) with 323 campsites at other locations; no reservations; Potwisha and South Fork open all year, other 2 open only in summer

2 campgrounds (see chart and map) with 60 campsites at Mineral King

Dorst Group Campground (see chart): 7 sites, each with 12-person minimum; reservations required; mid-June—Labor Day only

For those who seek a greater challenge, rock climbing is taught at some of the parks.

Giant Forest

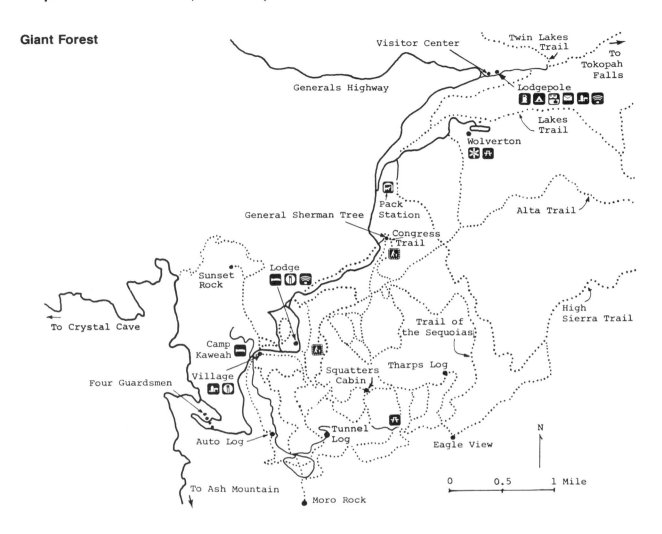

All state and national parks have standard rules and regulations, but some have special restrictions. See page I-14–I-10 for a brief summary.

limit of stay between June 14–Sept. 14 is 14 days; limit of stay between Sept. 15–June 13 is 30 days

Lodgepole and Potwisha Campgrounds have handicapped-accessible campsites

sanitary dump stations at Potwisha, open year-round; at Lodgepole and Dorst Campgrounds, open only May—Oct.

backcountry camping (June to November recommended): permit required; reservations accepted beginning March 1; half of permits available on a first-come, first-served basis

cabins/lodging at Giant Forest Village, Silver City and Stony Creek

fires permitted only in designated fire rings

picnicking

Mineral King

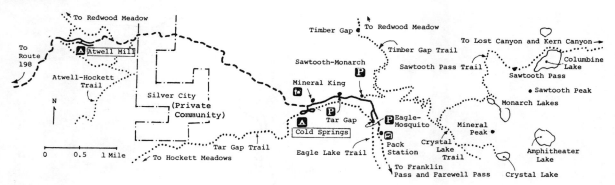

no motorcycles or bicycles allowed on trails; may be used only on roadways

horseback riding available at Wolverton pack station and Mineral King

fishing

hiking trails (over 800 miles in Sequoia and Kings Canyon combined)

self-guiding interpretive trails/exhibits

down-hill skiing at Wolverton snow play area (Friday–Sunday)

cross-country ski trails connect Giant Forest, Wolverton and Lodgepole Campground

Sequoia Ski Touring Center, in Giant Forest Village, operates daily during snow season

Visitor Centers at Lodgepole and Ash Mountain; Ranger Station at Mineral King

ranger-guided nature walks/evening campfires at Dorst, Potwisha and Lodgepole

post office at Lodgepole open year-round

food service, supplies, service station at Lodgepole, Giant Forest Village, Stony Creek and Silver City

pets must be on leash; not allowed on any park trails

the *Sequoia Bark*, the park's free newspaper, has current information on services and activities; available at Visitor Centers and entrance stations

Tent/RV Campgrounds	Elevation	Total Sites	RVs	Tents	Fee	Limit of Stay	Drinking Water	Flush Toilets	Sanitary Dump	Camp Store	Approx. Season
Atwell Mill	6,645	23	*	*	*	14	*				Memorial Day to late Sept.
Buckeye Flats	2,800	28		*	*	14	*	*			mid-April to mid-Oct.
Cold Springs	7,500	37	*	*	*	14	*			*	Memorial Day to late Sept.
Dorst	6,700	238	*	*	*	14	*	*	*	*	mid-June to Labor Day
Lodgepole	6,700	260	*	*	*	14	*	*	*	*	year-round
Potwisha	2,100	44	*	*	*	14	*	*	*		year-round
South Fork	3,600	13	*	*	*	14	*				year-round
Group Campground											
Dorst		7	*	*	*	14	*	*	*		mid-June to Labor Day
Backcountry Campsites											
Various locations (hike-in, horseback ride-in)		ltd		*							

Notes:

No trailers are allowed at Atwell Mill and Cold Springs Campgrounds.

South Fork Campground has no water in winter; not recommended for RVs and trailers.

Sierra National Forest

For Information

Forest Supervisor
Sierra National Forest
1600 Tollhouse Road
Clovis, CA 93611-0532
(209) 487-5155

Location

The Sierra National Forest lies east of Fresno in central California, and is west of the Sierra Nevada Crest between Yosemite and Sequoia-Kings Canyon National Parks. The road entry to the 1,412,641-acre forest is somewhat limited. No paved roads enter from the east or south. SH 41 crosses only a neck of forest road, making SH 168 the major entry road.

Special Notes

The Sierra National Forest is a varied land with brushy front country, dense forests, deep river canyons, many natural and man-made lakes, and glacial valleys. Elevations range from 900 feet to 13,986-foot Mt. Humphreys. The most popular and developed areas are at Bass Lake, Shaver Lake, Huntington Lake, Wishon Reservoir, Lake Edison, Dinkey Creek, and Mammoth Pool. There are more than 60 designated campgrounds and most of them are closed in the winter; openings begin in mid-April. A few campgrounds, at lower elevations, are open all year. Primary recreation attractions include camping, picnicking, boating, water skiing, swimming, fishing, and hiking.

The forest has two groves of Giant Sequoias: Nelder Grove and McKinley Grove. Nelder Grove, a 1,400-acre grove of Giant Sequoias, is located 10 miles north of Bass Lake in the Mariposa Ranger District. McKinley Grove has over 170 specimen-sized sequoias spread out over 100 acres. This grove is located in Kings River Ranger District five miles east of Dinkey Creek Campground on McKinley Grove Road.

Wintertime brings snowshoeing, snowmobiling, cross-country and downhill skiing and general snow play. Tamarack Ridge near Shaver Lake on SH 168 and Fish Camp along SH 41 are popular areas for cross-country skiing while Sierra Summit ski area near Huntington Lake provides downhill skiing. There are several snowmobiling trails in the forest.

More folks are enjoying the forest setting during the winter because of increased popularity of cross-country skiing and no crowds.

Wilderness Areas

The Sierra National Forest now contains approximately 528,000 acres of designated wilderness in five areas—Ansel Adams, Dinkey Lakes, John Muir, Kaiser, and Monarch.

Ansel Adams Wilderness, located in both the Sierra and Inyo National Forests, covers approximately 138,660 acres in the Sierra National Forest. Ansel Adams, formerly Minarets Wilderness, is characterized by spectacular alpine scenery with

REGION 5

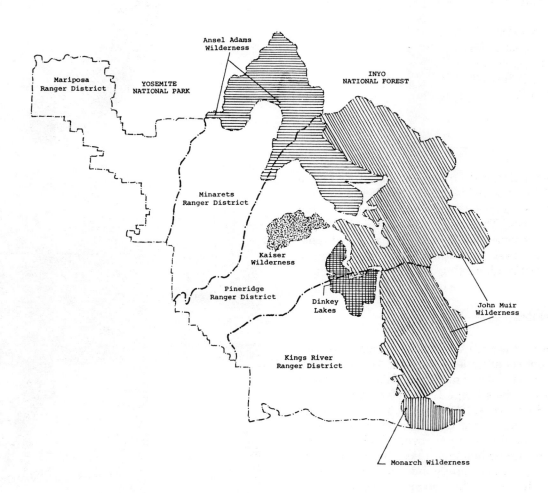

barren granite peaks, steep-walled gorges, and rock outcroppings. Elevations range from 3,500 feet to 13,157 feet.

Sixteen lakes are clustered in the west central region of the 30,000-acre *Dinkey Lakes Wilderness*. Most of the wilderness is above 8,000 feet. Vegetation is primarily lodgepole pine and there are many meadows and granite outcroppings.

The *John Muir Wilderness* covers 584,000 acres in the Sierra and Inyo National Forests. It is a land of snow-capped mountains with hundreds of lakes and streams and beautiful meadows. The higher elevations are barren granite with many glacially carved lakes.

The 22,700-acre *Kaiser Wilderness* provides a commanding view of the central Sierra Nevada from Kaiser Ridge. The top of the ridge is in the alpine zone. The descent from Kaiser Ridge into the northern part of the wilderness is quite abrupt.

The *Monarch Wilderness*, located in both the Sierra and Sequoia National Forests, is extremely rugged and difficult to traverse. Steep slopes extend up from the middle and main forks of the King River. Elevations range from 2,400 to over 10,000 feet. The Sierra National Forest portion of the wilderness is approximately 21,000 acres.

A Wilderness Visitor Permit is required for overnight trips into the John Muir, Kaiser, Ansel Adams, and Dinkey Lakes Wilderness areas. A quota system is in effect for the John Muir and Kaiser Wilderness areas and most of the Ansel Adams Wilderness from July 1 through Labor Day. The Pineridge Ranger District issues permits for the John Muir, Kaiser, Dinkey Lakes, and portions of Ansel Adams Wilderness. Minarets Ranger District issues permits to trailheads north of the middle fork of the San Joaquin River in the Ansel Adams Wilderness.

Sierra National Forest *(continued)*

Mariposa Ranger District

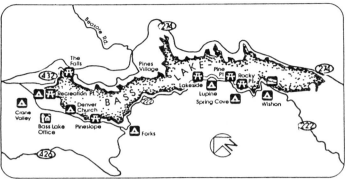

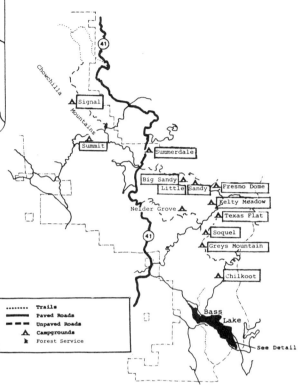

Campgrounds	Elevation (ft)	# of Units	Drinking Water	Toilets	Trailer Space	Fee Area
Big Sandy	5,800	14		P	4	
Chilcoot	4,600	12		P		
Forks	3,400	31	*	F	4	*
Fresno Dome	6,400	9		P	6	
Grey's Mountain	5,200	8		P		
Indian Flat	1,500	14	*	P	3	*
Jerseydale	3,600	10	*	P	2	
Kelty Meadow	5,800	10		P		
Little Sandy	6,100	8		P	2	
Lupine/Cedar	3,400	113	*	F	85	*
Nelder Grove	5,300	10		P	3	
Soquel	5,400	14		P		
Spring Cove	3,400	63	*	F	10	*
Summerdale	5,000	30	*	P	9	*
Summit Camp	5,800	10	*	P		
Wishon Point	3,400	47	*	V	24	*

Notes:
Bass Lake is accessible all year; at least 1 campground remains
open all year; November through April campground water sys-
tems must be turned off.
Dump station for self-contained RVs/trailers just off County Rd.
222 near the Forks Resort.
Reservations accepted through MISTIX for 4 campgrounds—
Forks, Lupine, Spring Cove, and Wishon Point.

For Information

Mariposa Ranger District
41969 Highway 41
Oakhurst, CA 93644
(209) 683-4665

Group Campgrounds

Crane Valley: at Bass Lake; 7 sites, each with 12–30
person maximum; no water, pit toilets; fee charged;
make reservations through MISTIX.
Jerseydale: used as a group campground outside of
normal season; water, vault toilets; first-come,
first-served.
Youth Group at Recreation Point, Bass Lake: 4 sites,
each with 20–30 person maximum; water, flush
toilets; fee charged; make reservations through
MISTIX.
Texas Flat: on Skyranch Road north of Bass Lake;
4 sites, each with 20–30 person maximum; creek
water, pit toilets; first-come, first-served.

Sierra National Forest *(continued)*

Minarets Ranger District

Campgrounds	Elevation (ft)	# of Units	Drinking Water	Toilets	Trailer Space	Fee Area
China Bar	3,300	6		P		
Clover Meadow	7,000	7		P	7	
Fish Creek	4,600	7		P		
Gaggs Camp	5,700	9		P		
Granite Creek	7,000	20		P		
Little Jackass	4,800	5		P		
Lower Chiquito	4,900	7		P		
Mammoth Pool	3,500	47	*	P	30	
Placer	4,100	7	*	P		
Rock Creek	4,300	19	*	P	13	
Soda Springs	4,300	16		P	7	
Sweet Water	3,800	10		P	7	
Upper Chiquito	6,800	20		P		

Note:
China Bar Campground is accessible by boat only.

Group Campground

Bowler: located on Beasore Road; 6 sites, each with 30 person maximum; no water, pit toilets; no fee; no reservations required.

For Information

Minarets Ranger District
North Fork, CA 93643
(209) 877-2218

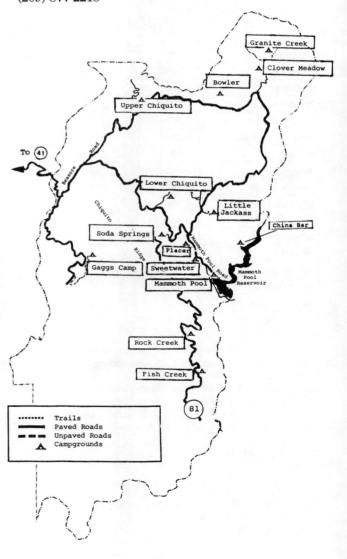

You can bet that fence is not keeping that doe in or out!

Sierra National Forest *(continued)*

Pineridge Ranger District

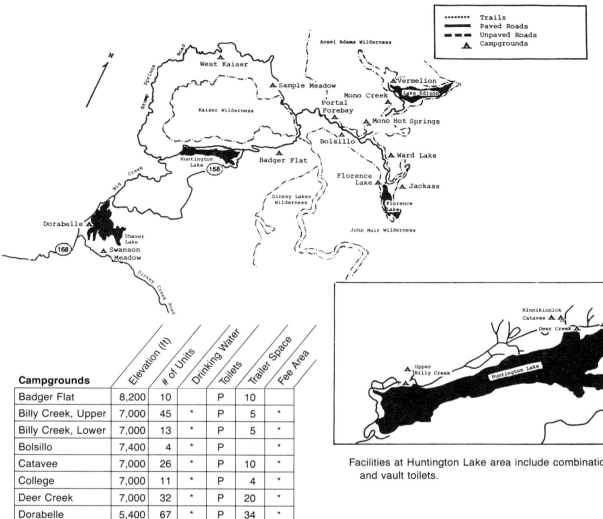

Campgrounds	Elevation (ft)	# of Units	Drinking Water	Toilets	Trailer Space	Fee Area
Badger Flat	8,200	10		P	10	
Billy Creek, Upper	7,000	45	*	P	5	*
Billy Creek, Lower	7,000	13	*	P	5	*
Bolsillo	7,400	4	*	P		*
Catavee	7,000	26	*	P	10	*
College	7,000	11	*	P	4	*
Deer Creek	7,000	32	*	P	20	*
Dorabelle	5,400	67	*	P	34	*
Florence Lake	7,400	14		P		
Jackass Meadow	7,200	50	*	P		*
Kinnikinnick	7,000	32	*	P	16	*
Mono Creek	7,400	16	*	P		*
Mono Hot Springs	6,500	31	*	P		*
Portal Forebay	7,200	9	*	P		*
Rancheria	7,000	150	*	P	67	*
Sample Meadow	7,800	16		P	16	
Swanson Meadow	5,600	12		P	10	
Vermillion	7,700	30	*	P		*
Ward Lake	7,300	17		P		
West Kaiser		10		P		

Notes:
Normal open season for all campgrounds is June through September, except Dorabelle and Swanson Meadow are open May through September.

Facilities at Huntington Lake area include combination of flush and vault toilets.

For Information

Pineridge Ranger District
P.O. Box 300
Shaver Lake, CA 93664
(209) 841-3311

Group Campgrounds

Badger Flat: located east of Huntington Lake; fee charged; 100 person maximum; reservations through ranger district office.

Midge Creek: located east of Huntington Lake; fee charged; 2 sites, each with 50 person maximum; reservations through ranger district office.

Kings River Ranger District

Campgrounds	Elevation (ft)	# of Units	Drinking Water	Toilets	Trailer Space	Fee Area
Black Rock	4,200	7		P	1	*
Buck Meadow	6,800	10		P	5	
Dinkey Creek	5,700	158	*	P/F	47	*
Gigantea	6,500	7		P	5	
Kirch Flat	1,100	24		P	16	
Lily Pad	6,500	16		P	10	
Marmot Rock	8,200	10		P		
Sawmill Flat	6,700	15		P	10	
Sycamore I	1,200	12		P	12	
Sycamore II	1,200	20		P	20	
Trapper Springs	8,200	30	*	P	30	*
Voyager Rock	8,200	14		P		

Notes:
Lily Pad, Marmot Rock and Trapper Springs Campgrounds are operated by Pacific Gas & Electric.
Dinkey Creek Campground is operated by West Valley College, with reservations through Mistix.

For Information

Kings River Ranger District
34849 Maxon Road
Sanger, CA 93657
(209) 855-8321

Group Campgrounds

Dinkey Creek Group Campground: 30–45 persons; water and toilets; fee charged; reservations at (408) 867-2200.

Sycamore I: located at Pine Flat Reservoir; 120 person maximum; no drinking water, toilets; no fee; reservations at Kings River Ranger District office.

Kirch Flat: on upper Kings River; 50 persons maximum; no drinking water, pit toilets; fee charged; reservations at Kings River Ranger District office.

Green Cabin (100 max.), Mill Flat (50 max.), and Gravel Flat (200 max.): all located on upper Kings River; groups must provide toilet facilities and drinking water; no fee; reservations required at Kings River Ranger District office.

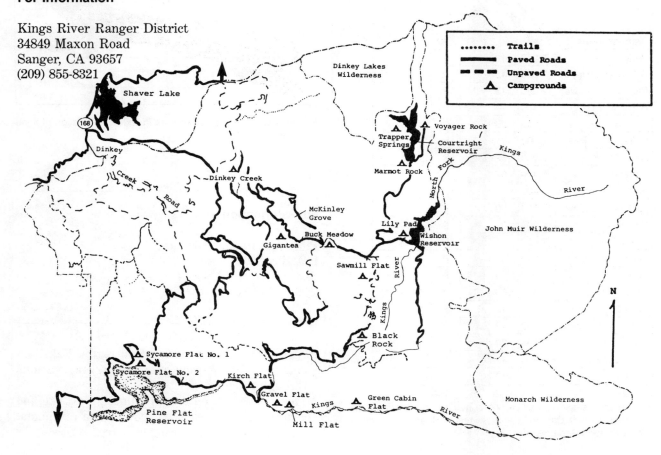

Success Lake

For Information

Corps of Engineers
Success Lake
P.O. Box 1072
Porterville, CA 93258
(209) 784-0215

Location

Success Lake is located on the Tule River 8 miles east of the city of Porterville in the Sierra Nevada Foothills. There is a 1,400-acre wildlife area that makes up about one-third of the total park area. In the spring and summer months high water covers shoreline vegetation, which makes for excellent shoreline angling.

Statistics

2,450 acres, surface area
3.5 miles long
30 miles of shoreline

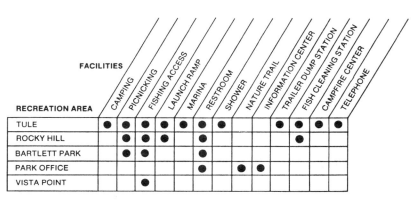

RECREATION AREA	CAMPING	PICNICKING	FISHING ACCESS	LAUNCH RAMP	MARINA	RESTROOM	SHOWER	NATURE TRAIL	INFORMATION CENTER	TRAILER DUMP STATION	FISH CLEANING STATION	CAMPFIRE CENTER	TELEPHONE
TULE	●	●	●	●	●	●	●		●	●	●	●	●
ROCKY HILL		●	●	●		●				●			
BARTLETT PARK		●	●			●							
PARK OFFICE						●		●	●				
VISTA POINT			●										

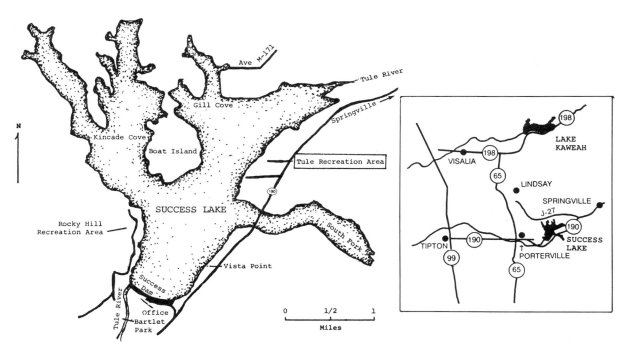

Turlock Lake State Recreation Area

For Information

Turlock Lake State Recreation Area
22600 Lake Road
La Grange, CA 95329
(209) 874-2008

Location

Turlock Lake State Recreation Area is located 25 miles east of Modesto off of Highway 132. To reach the 408-acre park, turn south from Highway 132 onto Roberts Ferry Road, go one mile to Lake Road and turn east. At an elevation of 248 feet, the recreation area features the 3,500-surface-acre lake containing some 26 miles of shoreline. It is in Stanislaus County.

Special Notes

This is an ideal setting for water-oriented outdoor recreation, bounded on the north by the Tuolumne River and on the south by the lake. The recreation area boasts typical San Joaquin Valley weather, with warm summers and mild winters.

Facilities & Activities

66 developed campsites
showers
24-foot trailers; 27-foot campers/motorhomes
picnicking
fishing
hiking trails
swimming
boating (launch ramp, mooring, water skiing)
food service
supplies
on State Park Reservation System
  (mid-May—mid-Sept.)

The perfect location—a campsite by a bubbling stream.

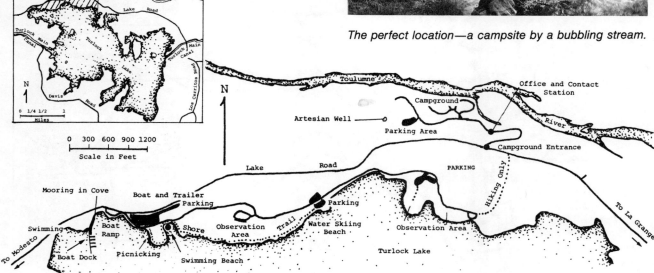

Yosemite National Park

For Information

Superintendent
P.O. Box 577
Yosemite National Park
Yosemite National Park, CA 95389
(209) 372-0200
(209) 372-0264 for general park information

Location

Yosemite National Park embraces more than 760,000 acres of scenic wildlands set aside in 1890 to preserve a portion of the Sierra Nevada Mountains that stretch along California's eastern flank. Access to Yosemite is via SH 140 and 120 eastbound from Merced and Manteca; SH 41 northbound from Fresno; and SH 120 westbound from Lee Vining (closed in winter). The park offers 3 major features: alpine wilderness, groves of Giant Sequoias, and Yosemite Valley.

Special Notes

The *Tuolumne Meadows* section of Yosemite has some of the most rugged, sublime scenery in the Sierra. The Tioga Road (SH 120) crosses this area. This scenic highway passes through an area of sparkling lakes, meadows, domes, and lofty peaks. At Tioga Pass the road crosses the Sierra's crest at 9,945 feet, the highest automobile pass in California. Tuolumne Meadows, at 8,600 feet is the largest subalpine meadow in the Sierra. It is 55 miles from Yosemite Valley via the Tioga Road. In the summer, Tuolumne Meadows is a favorite starting point for backpacking trips and day hikes. It is also growing in popularity as a winter mountaineering area.

Yosemite Valley is characterized by sheer walls and a flat floor. "The Incomparable Valley," so it has been called, is probably the world's best known example of a glacier-carved canyon, its leaping waterfalls, towering cliffs, rounded domes, and massive monoliths make it a preeminent natural marvel. Around the valley's perimeter, waterfalls, which reach their maximum flow in May and June, crash to the floor. Yosemite, Bridalveil, Vernal, Nevada, and Illilouette are the most prominent of these falls, some of which have little or no water from mid-August through early fall.

Glacier Point is one of those rare places where the scenery is so vast that it overwhelms the viewer. It affords you a bird's-eye view the length and breadth of Yosemite Valley. Across the valley you can see the entire 2,425-foot drop of Yosemite Falls. The road to Glacier Point, a 32-mile drive from Yosemite Valley, is closed in the winter beyond the ski area at Summit Meadow.

The *Mariposa Grove*, 35 miles south of Yosemite Valley, is the largest of three Sequoia groves in Yosemite. The Tuolumne and Merced Groves are near Crane Flat. The Mariposa Grove's Grizzly Giant is 2,700 years old and is thought to be the oldest

(text continued on page 95)

You can enjoy Yosemite's unparalled beauty on more than 700 miles of trails ranging from easy one-day hikes to rigorous multi-day treks.

REGION 5

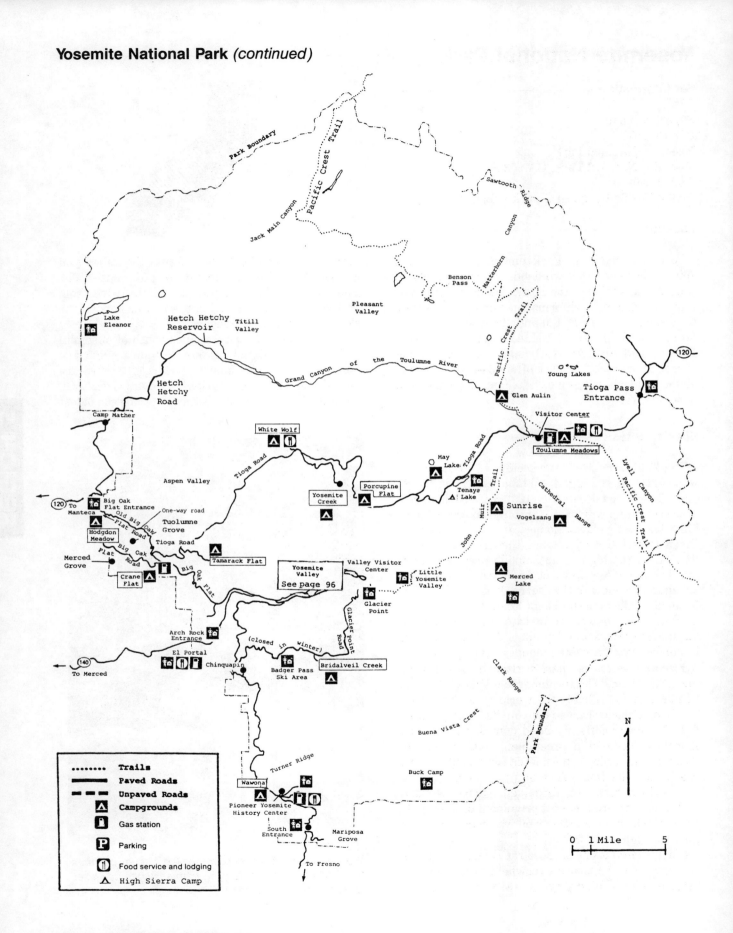

Yosemite National Park *(continued)*

Campgrounds/ General Location	Elevation (ft)	Miles from Yosemite Valley	# of Units	RV space	Drinking water	Toilets	Pets allowed	Camping season (approximate)
North Pines (R) Yosemite Valley	4,000	0	86	*	*	F		May–Oct
Upper Pines (R) Yosemite Valley	4,000	0	240	*	*	F	*	Apr–Nov
Lower Pines (R) Yosemite Valley	4,000	0	173	*	*	F		all year
Upper River (R) Yosemite Valley	4,000	0	124		*	F		May–Oct
Lower River (R) Yosemite Valley	4,000	0	139	*	*	F		May–Oct
Sunnyside Walk-In Yosemite Valley	4,000	0	38		*	F		all year
Backpackers Walk-In Yosemite Valley	4,000	0	25		*	F		May–Oct
Wawona Highway 41 in Wawona	4,000	27	100	*	*	F	*	all year
Bridalveil Creek Glacier Point Road	7,200	27	110	*	*	F	*	Jun–Sept
Hodgdon Meadow (R) Highway 120 west near Big Oak Flat	4,872	25	107	*	*	F	*	all year
Crane Flat (R) Highway 120 west near the Tioga Road turnoff	6,190	17	129	*	*	F	*	Jun–Oct
Tamarack Flat Highway 120 east	6,315	23	52	*	str.	P		Jun–Oct
White Wolf Highway 120 east	8,000	31	87	*	*	F	*	Jun–Oct
Yosemite Creek Highway 120 east	7,659	35	75	*	str.	P		Jun–Oct
Porcupine Flat Highway 120 east	8,100	38	52	*	str.	P		Jun–Oct
Tenaya Lake Walk-In Highway 120 east, west end of Tenaya Lake	7,600	46	50		*	F		Jun–Oct
Tuolumne Meadows (R) Highway 120 east, Tuolumne Meadows	8,600	55	325	*	*	F	*	Jun–Oct

Notes:

R = Mistix reservations required approximately May–Sept. for North Pines, Upper Pines, Lower Pines, Upper River, Lower River, Hodgdon Meadow, Tuolumne Meadows, and Crane Flat.

For backpackers/visitors without vehicles, 2-night max. for Backpackers Walk-In Campground.

3-mile access road not suitable for large RVs or trailers for Tamarack Flat Campground.

5-mile access road not suitable for large RVs or trailers for Yosemite Creek Campground.

REGION 5

RV access to front section only for Porcupine Flat Campground.

25 walk-in spaces available for backpackers/visitors without vehicles ($1/person) for Tuolumne Meadows Campground.

All campgrounds have tent space, tables, fire pits or grills, and all require a fee.

Dump stations are located at Upper Pines, Lower River, and Tuolumne Meadows Campgrounds.

Group Campgrounds	# of Units	Limit of stay	Drinking water	Toilets	Camping season
Bridalveil Creek (walk-in)	1	14	*	F	Jun—Sept
Hodgdon Meadow (walk-in)	5	14	*	F	Memorial Day—Sept
Tuolumne Meadows (walk-in)	8	14	*	F	July—Labor Day
Wawona (walk-in)	1	14	*	F	mid-May—Sept
Yosemite Valley (walk-in)	11	7	*	F	mid-May—Sept

Notes:

Reservations required through Ranger Station District Office for Bridalveil Creek, Tuolumne Meadows, and Wawona Campgrounds.

Mistix reservations required for Yosemite Valley Campground.

All campgrounds have tent space and require a fee.

The U-shape of Yosemite Valley indicates it was carved out by a glacier thousands of years ago.

Yosemite National Park *(continued)*

(text continued from page 91)
of all Sequoias. You can ride the trams throughout the Grove from about May 1 to October 15, and you can use the trails year round for either hiking or for cross-country skiing.

The park ranges from 2,000 feet above sea level to more than 13,000 feet. Within its boundaries are more than 200 lakes, 550 miles of streams, 750 miles of hiking trails, 90 miles of cross-country skiing trails, and 200 miles of roads. Yosemite is truly a park for all seasons. Although the backcountry is not vehicle-accessible between about mid-November until late May, the valley is open year-round. Each season has something special to offer.

Facilities & Activities

park entrance fee

camping permitted only in designated campgrounds

7 campgrounds (see chart) in Yosemite Valley with 825 campsites: 5 of these on Ticketron reservation system, approx. May—Sept.; first-come, first-served basis at other times; 7-day camping limit from June 1—Sept. 15; 30-day camping limit from Sept. 16—May 31

10 campgrounds (see chart) outside Yosemite Valley with 1,087 campsites: first-come, first-served basis at all times; 14-day camping limit from June 1—Sept. 15; 30-day camping limit from Sept. 16—May 31

5 group campgrounds (see chart): for groups of 10–30 persons

no utility hookups for trailers/RVs

backcountry camping: wilderness permits required; free; submit request between Feb. 1 and May 31; backcountry is on a trailhead quota system and 50% of each trailhead's quota is available by reservation, remaining 50% available on first-come, first-served basis

food should be hung high in the backcountry to avoid attracting bears

campfires permitted only at designated campsites; dead and down trees and limbs may be used for firewood

picnicking

self-guiding nature trails

hiking/backpacking trails (over 750 miles in park; 35 miles in Valley)

bicycle trails/rentals (Valley)

horseback riding/guided trail rides from Yosemite, Wawona, Tuolumne Meadows and White Wolf

swimming: pools at Curry Village and Yosemite Lodge in season; permitted at all lakes and streams except when posted

fishing

boating/canoeing/rafting (non-motorized) permitted only at Tenaya Lake, Merced Lake, May Lake and Merced River between Lower Pines Campground and El Capitan Bridge; raft rentals available in season at Curry Village

rock climbing (climbers should register at closest Ranger Station)

climbing lessons available at Yosemite Mountaineering School

cross-country skiing

snowshoeing

Geologists surmise that as the glacier crept along, it sheared away Half Dome's other half.

YOSEMITE VALLEY

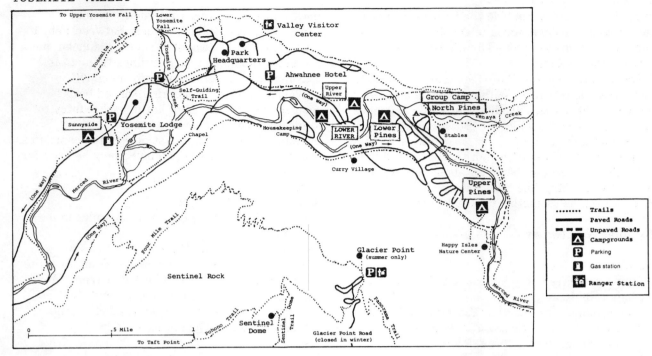

These picnic tables in Yosemite Valley won't be empty in summer. Try to visit in April or May before the summer "crunch."

ice skating (approx. Thanksgiving to mid-March) at outdoor ice rink at Curry Village

alpine skiing at Badger Pass (beginner and intermediate)

skiing lessons available at Yosemite Ski School

shuttlebus service in Yosemite Valley year-round

road touring (descriptive booklet available)

bus tours from Yosemite Valley

tram rides in Mariposa Grove

eating facilities, stores and lodging available at: Yosemite Valley, Wawona, El Portal, Tuolumne Meadows and White Wolf

showers at Curry Housekeeping (Valley) from early spring through fall; White Wolf and Tuolumne Meadows Lodges in summer

museums/interpretive exhibits

several visitor centers; principal one at Yosemite Valley

campfire programs/park naturalists programs/guided walks/seminars

pets must be kept on leash; not allowed on trails, beaches, or backcountry; campers with pets are restricted to specific campgrounds; boarding kennel is available at Yosemite Valley Stables

Yosemite Guide, a free newspaper, has current park information and is available at entrance stations, ranger stations and visitor centers

all natural and historic features are protected

REGION 6

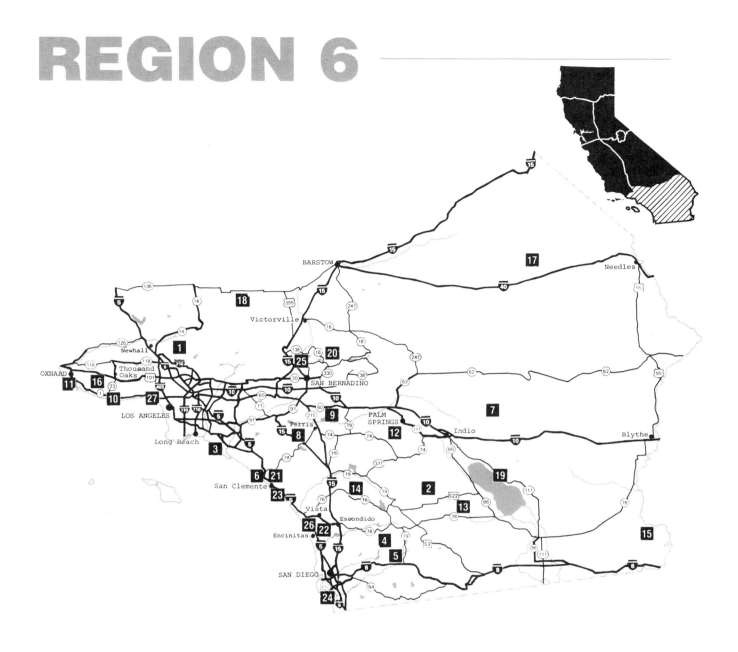

BARSTOW
Needles
Victorville
Newhall
OXNARD
Thousand Oaks
LOS ANGELES
Long Beach
San Clemente
Vista
Encinitas
Escondido
SAN BERNADINO
PALM SPRINGS
Perris
Indio
Blythe
SAN DIEGO

1—Angeles National Forest, 98
2—Anza-Borrego Desert State Park, 104
3—Bolsa Chica State Beach, 124
4—Cleveland National Forest, 106
5—Cuyamaca Rancho State Park, 110
6—Doheny State Beach, 124
7—Joshua Tree National Monument, 112
8—Lake Elsinore State Park, 114
9—Lake Perris State Recreation Area, 115
10—Leo Carillo State Beach, 117
11—McGrath State Beach, 118
12—Mount San Jacinto State Park and Wilderness, 120
13—Ocotillo Wells State Vehicular Recreation Area, 122
14—Palomar Mountain State Park, 126

15—Picacho State Recreation Area, 127
16—Point Mugu State Park, 128
17—Providence Mountains State Recreation Area, 129
18—Saddleback Butte State Park, 130
19—Salton Sea State Recreation Area, 131
20—San Bernardino National Forest, 132
21—San Clemente State Beach, 125
22—San Elijo State Beach, 139
23—San Onofre State Beach, 140
24—Silver Strand State Beach, 141
25—Silverwood Lake State Recreation Area, 142
26—South Carlsbad State Beach, 139
27—Topanga State Park, 143

REGION 6

Angeles National Forest

For Information

Forest Supervisor
Angeles National Forest
701 North Santa Anita Avenue
Arcadia, CA 91006
(818) 574-5200

Location

The Angeles National Forest is located just north of the Los Angeles Basin in two sections from the Ventura County line on the west to the San Bernardino County line on the east. The steep, rugged 693,000-acre forest covers about one-fourth of Los Angeles County land. Elevations range from 1,200 to 10,164 feet.

Special Notes

The forest serves as a watershed and recreation zone for the Los Angeles area. Scenic drives through the forest provide wonderful views all year. Portions of the forest may be closed during fire season, generally from June through November. Most campgrounds are open year-round, but some are closed in the winter.

The gentle slopes of the Saugus District are especially beautiful when colored with wildflowers in the spring. The Pyramid and Castaic reservoirs provide for boating, fishing, skiing, and swimming, while San Gabriel Reservoir has excellent fishing. The desert slopes of the Tunjunga and Valyermo districts are excellent exhibits of the tremendous geologic forces that shaped these mountains.

There are hundreds of miles of trails in the Angeles National Forest: nature, hiking, backpacking, and equestrian. The Pacific Crest Trail enters the forest near Wright Mountain and southeast of Guffy Campground. You can pick it up from many places along the Angeles Crest Highway. It crosses the Saugus Ranger District and exits to the north, some 180 miles later.

Visitor centers are located at Chilao, Big Pines, and Crystal Lake. The centers are an excellent beginning for your visit as they offer an introduction to the forest as well as providing information that will be useful for your trip. There are six downhill ski areas in the forest. Each area is unique, offering a different level of development and skiing experience. Cross-country skiing on the unplowed forest roads is also popular in the winter.

Wilderness Areas

Three Wilderness Areas in the forest offer the experienced hiker vast areas for exploration. The

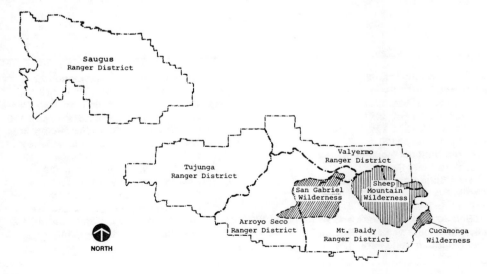

Angeles National Forest *(continued)*

36,118-acre *San Gabriel Wilderness* encompasses some extremely rugged terrain, ranging in elevation from 1,600 to 8,200 feet. Five trails are maintained and you can enter the wilderness via one of three trails: Bear Creek, Mt. Waterman, and Devil's Canyon.

Sheep Mountain Wilderness has extremely rugged terrain. Mt. Baldy at 10,064 feet elevation is the highest peak in the San Gabriel Mountains. A small portion of the 43,600-acre wilderness area is in the San Bernardino Forest. A wilderness permit is required for entry from the East Fork Trailhead only.

The Chapman Trail from Ice House Canyon provides access into the *Cucamonga Wilderness* from Angeles National Forest. About one-third of the wilderness area, some 4,400 acres, is in the Angeles National Forest, with 8,581 acres in the San Bernardino Forest. A visitor permit is required prior to entering; the quota system is used and reservations are advised during the heavy use season.

Mt. Baldy Ranger District

Campgrounds	Elevation (ft)	# of Units	Drinking Water	Toilets	Trailer Space	Fee Area
Coldbrook	3,350	25	*	V	*	*
Crystal Lake	5,600	176	*	F	*	*
Deer Flats Group			*	F		*
Glenn Trail Camp	2,000	10	str.	V		
Little Jimmy Trail Camp	7,500	8	spr.	V		
Manker Flats	6,300	20	*	F	*	*

Notes:
Reservations required at Deer Flats Group Campground; phone (818) 910-1161; campground can accommodate 20–500 persons; usually closed in winter.

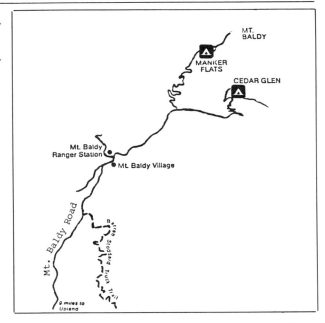

For Information

Mt. Baldy Ranger District
110 North Wabash Avenue
Glendora, CA 91740
(818) 335-1251

REGION 6

Valyermo Ranger District

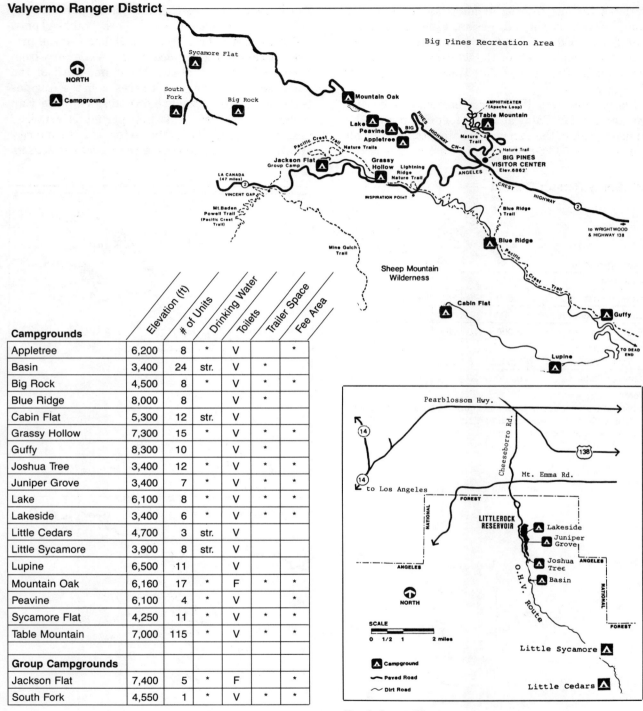

Campgrounds	Elevation (ft)	# of Units	Drinking Water	Toilets	Trailer Space	Fee Area
Appletree	6,200	8	*	V		*
Basin	3,400	24	str.	V	*	
Big Rock	4,500	8	*	V	*	*
Blue Ridge	8,000	8		V	*	
Cabin Flat	5,300	12	str.	V		
Grassy Hollow	7,300	15	*	V	*	*
Guffy	8,300	10		V	*	
Joshua Tree	3,400	12	*	V	*	*
Juniper Grove	3,400	7	*	V	*	*
Lake	6,100	8	*	V	*	*
Lakeside	3,400	6	*	V	*	*
Little Cedars	4,700	3	str.	V		
Little Sycamore	3,900	8	str.	V		
Lupine	6,500	11		V		
Mountain Oak	6,160	17	*	F	*	*
Peavine	6,100	4	*	V		*
Sycamore Flat	4,250	11	*	V	*	*
Table Mountain	7,000	115	*	V	*	*
Group Campgrounds						
Jackson Flat	7,400	5	*	F		*
South Fork	4,550	1	*	V	*	*

Notes:

Jackson Flat Group Camp (3 sites with 40 persons max. each; 2 sites with 30 persons max. each) requires advance registration; phone (619) 249-3483.

South Fork Group Camp (50 persons max.) requires advance registration through Valyermo Ranger District office.

For Information

Valyermo Ranger District
P.O. Box 15
Valyermo, CA 93563
(805) 944-2187

Angeles National Forest *(continued)*

Arroyo Seco Ranger District

Campgrounds	Elevation (ft)	Piped Water	Stream Water	Toilets	Fee
Buckhorn	6,300	*	*	*	*
Chilao	5,200	*		*	*
Horse Flats	5,800	*		*	*
Millard	1,900	*	*	*	
Mt. Pacifico	7,100			*	
Sulphur Springs	5,200	*		*	*
Valley Forge	3,500	*	*	*	
West Fork	3,100	*	*	*	*
Trail Camps					
Bear Canyon	3,400		*	*	
Cooper Canyon	6,300		*	*	
De Vore	3,000		*		
Hoeges	2,500		*	*	
Idlehour	2,500				
Mt. Lowe	4,500	*	*	*	
Oakwilde	1,800		*	*	
Spruce Grove	3,100		*	*	
Group Campgrounds					
Bandido	5,700	*		*	*
Coulter	5,200	*		*	*

Notes:
Coulter Group Campground, near Chilao Campground, (50 persons max.); Bandido Group Campground (2 sites for 60 each max. or 1 site for 120 max.); advance registration required, phone (818) 578-1079.

Chilao Campground has 115 sites for RVs and trailers; no hook-ups.

Dump station is located at Charlton Flat.

Most campgrounds are closed from December to April but Chilao Campground keeps 30 spaces open year-round.

For Information

Arroyo Seco Ranger District
Oak Grove Park
Flintridge, CA 91011
(818) 790-1151

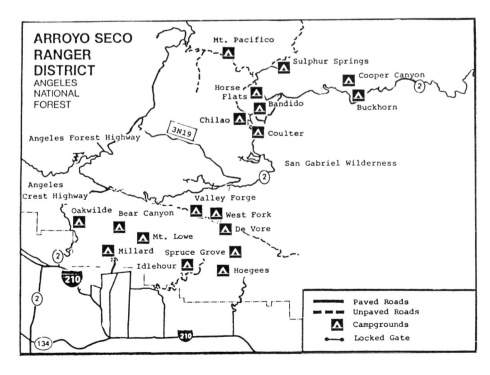

REGION 6

Angeles National Forest *(continued)*

Tujunga Ranger District

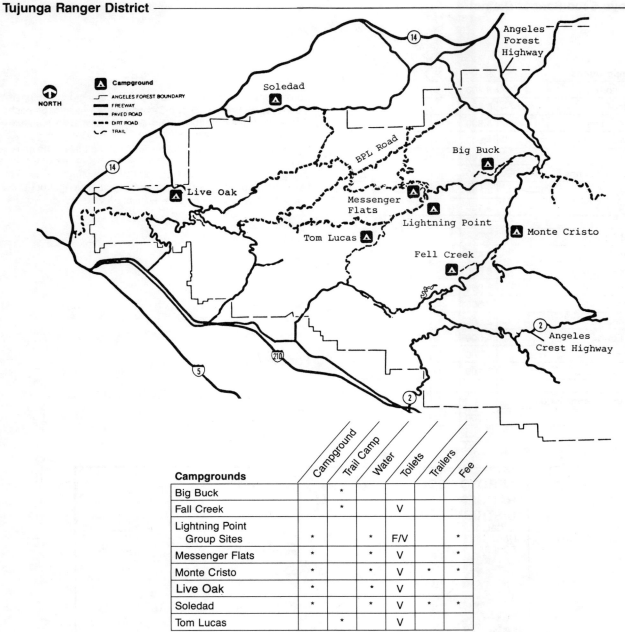

Campgrounds	Campground	Trail Camp	Water	Toilets	Trailers	Fee
Big Buck		*				
Fall Creek		*	V			
Lightning Point Group Sites	*		*	F/V		*
Messenger Flats	*		*	V		*
Monte Cristo	*		*	V	*	*
Live Oak	*		*	V		
Soledad	*		*	V	*	*
Tom Lucas		*		V		

Notes:
Round Top and Lightning Point Group Sites are closed in the
   winter.
Lightning Point Group Sites are by reservations only through the
   district ranger office.

For Information

Tujunga Ranger District
12371 North Little Tujunga Canyon Road
San Fernando, CA 91342
(818) 899-1900

Angeles National Forest *(continued)*

Saugus Ranger District

Campgrounds	Elevation (ft)	# of Units	Drinking Water	Toilets	Trailer Space	Fee Area
Bear	5,400	8		V		
Big Oak	2,240	9	*	V		*
Boquet	2,240	4	*	V		*
Cienaga	2,000	16		V		
Cottonwood	2,680	22	*	V	*	*
Hardluck	2,600	22	*	V	*	*
Los Alamos	2,600	93	*	F	*	*
Oak Flat	2,800	27	*	V	*	*
Prospect	2,150	22	*	F		*
Sawmill	5,200	8		V	*	
South Portal	2,700	10		V	*	
Streamside	2,300	9	*	V		*
Zuni	1,700	10		V		
Group Campground						
Los Alamos Group	2,600	3	*	V	*	*

Notes:
Prospect and Streamside are closed in the winter.

Sawmill, South Portal and Cienaga Campgrounds are accessible by dirt road, which may be impassable during winter months.

Los Alamos Group Campground (3 sites, 25 max. each) requires advance registration through the Saugus Ranger District office.

For Information

Saugus Ranger District
30800 Boquet Canyon Road
Saugus, CA 91350
(805) 296-9710

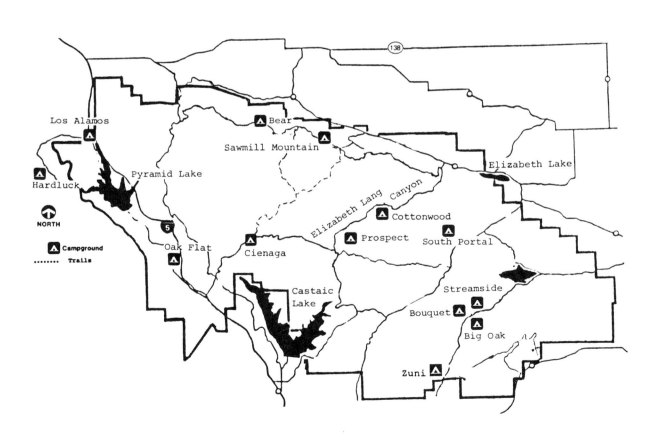

Anza-Borrego Desert State Park

For Information

Anza-Borrego Desert State Park
200 Palm Canyon Drive
Borrego Springs, CA 92004
(619) 767-5311

Location

Anza-Borrego Desert State Park is located approximately 85 miles northeast of San Diego via I-8, Highways 79 and 78. Located in Imperial and San Diego Counties, the 600,000 acres of spectacular dunes, washes, wildflowers, palm groves, cacti, and dramatic sweeping vistas make this the largest state park in the continental United States. Elevations range from 15 feet to 6,193 feet.

Facilities & Activities

2 developed campgrounds: Borrego Palm Canyon and Tamarisk Grove
  65 developed sites at Borrego Palm Canyon for tents, 24-foot trailers and 31-foot campers/motorhomes
  52 full hookup campsites for RVs at Borrego Palm Canyon for 35-foot trailers/campers/motorhomes
  campsites for disabled and solar showers at Borrego Palm Canyon
  25 developed sites at Tamarisk Grove for 21-foot trailers/campers/motorhomes
  campsites for disabled and solar showers at Tamarisk Grove
10 primitive campgrounds/camping areas in isolated park areas (see chart for details)
environmental campsites in Blair Valley; walk-in (100 yards); bring own water; pit toilets
open camping allowed almost anywhere in park
5 group camps at Borrego Palm Canyon (each with 24 person/6 vehicle max.); developed; solar showers; no trailers/campers/RVs; limited parking; can reserve all 5 for a total of 120
equestrian camping (10 sites); must have at least 1 horse per site; maximum of 3 horses per corral per site; 30 corrals; trailer in; lots of trailer space; primitive camping; chemical toilets; solar heated showers; 24-foot trailers/campers/motorhomes; water available
picnicking
hiking trails
nature trails
exhibits
horseback riding trails
Borrego Palm Canyon, Tamarisk Grove, group camps, and Horseman's Camp all on State Park Reservation System (Oct.—May)

Special Notes

"Borrego" refers to the desert bighorn sheep that live in the park's mountains. The best time to enjoy the wildflowers, palm groves, cacti, and other wonders is usually March and April. Vehicles should travel only on designated routes, either the paved or the park's 500-plus miles of primitive roads. Cross-country travel damages the desert plants.

Anza-Borrego Desert is the only California state park where visitors may camp outside regular campgrounds. Backpackers should camp a couple of hundred yards from water sources, so that wildlife can reach the water, and vehicle campers should park no more than a car's length from the roadway. Use only camp stoves (no ground fires) and carry out your garbage.

Deserts have as much beauty and majesty as other parks—they just take more patience and keener perception to appreciate.

Anza-Borrego Desert State Park *(continued)*

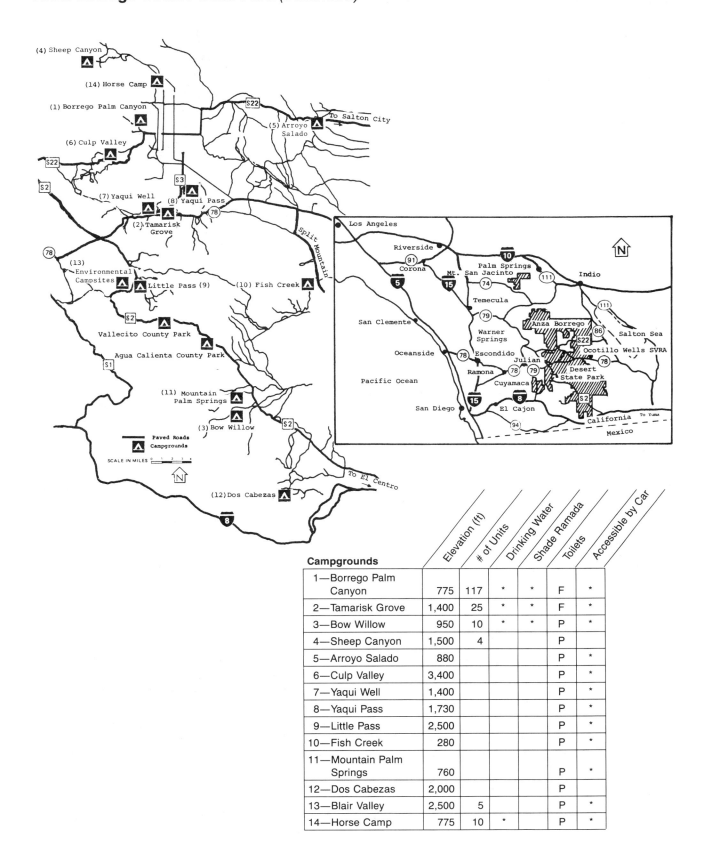

Campgrounds	Elevation (ft)	# of Units	Drinking Water	Shade Ramada	Toilets	Accessible by Car
1—Borrego Palm Canyon	775	117	*	*	F	*
2—Tamarisk Grove	1,400	25	*	*	F	*
3—Bow Willow	950	10	*	*	P	*
4—Sheep Canyon	1,500	4			P	
5—Arroyo Salado	880				P	*
6—Culp Valley	3,400				P	*
7—Yaqui Well	1,400				P	*
8—Yaqui Pass	1,730				P	*
9—Little Pass	2,500				P	*
10—Fish Creek	280				P	*
11—Mountain Palm Springs	760				P	*
12—Dos Cabezas	2,000				P	
13—Blair Valley	2,500	5			P	*
14—Horse Camp	775	10	*		P	*

Cleveland National Forest

For Information

Forest Supervisor
Cleveland National Forest
10845 Rancho Bernardo Road Suite 200
San Diego, CA 92127-2107
(619) 673-6180

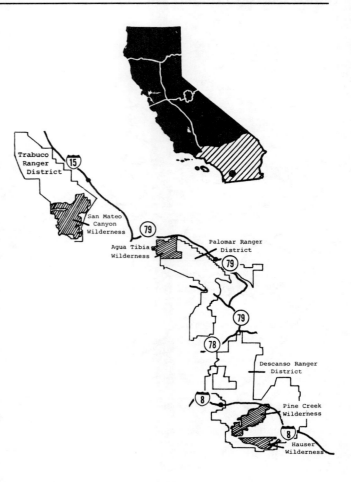

Location

The Cleveland National Forest comprises three non-contiguous land areas along the west coast of southern California totaling 566,850 acres. The forest, located in San Diego, Orange, and Riverside counties extends from within 5 miles of the Mexican border northward 135 miles to the Los Angeles Basin. It ranges from 6 to 60 miles from the Pacific Ocean and is about a one-hour drive from San Diego.

Special Notes

The topography of the Cleveland National Forest varies from boulder-strewn hills covered with chaparral to mile-high mountains with plateau tops where coniferous forest prevails. The forest has a true semi-arid Mediterranean climate. It is also, by nature, a forest of fire. Annually, in the fall, hot easterly winds, known as Santa Anas, blow with gale force intensity causing extreme, burning conditions. For public safety and resource protection *open fires in the Cleveland National Forest are restricted* and fire regulations are in effect all year.

A marvelous way to enjoy some spectacular scenery, but you better want to go with the wind.

Wilderness Areas

Four Wilderness Areas are in the Cleveland National Forest. *San Mateo Canyon Wilderness* (approximately 39,540 acres) is in the southern section in the Trabuco Ranger District. Terrain is moderate to steep; vegetation is chaparral on slopes, riparian in stream channels, and oak woodland at lower elevations.

Agua Tibia Wilderness (15,933 acres) is in the northwest section in the Palomar Ranger District. Elevations range from 1,700 to 5,000 feet. Best travel time is winter through spring as water is scarce and summer temperatures exceed 100°.

Pine Creek Wilderness (approximately 13,000 acres) and *Hauser Wilderness* (approximately 8,000 acres) are in the southern section in Descanso Ranger District. Gently sloping areas in Pine Creek range from 2,000 feet in the south to 4,000 feet in the north. All streams are dry for parts of the year. Hauser has mountainous terrain with steep slopes. Granite boulders and rock outcrops are common. Elevation ranges from 1,600 feet to 3,681 feet.

Cleveland National Forest *(continued)*

Trabuco Ranger District

Campgrounds	Elevation (ft)	# of Units	Drinking Water	Toilets	Trailer Space	Fee Area
Bluejay	3,400	51	*	V	*	*
El Cariso North	2,600	24	*	V	*	*
El Cariso South	2,600	19	*	V	*	*
*Tenaja	2,000	5	*	V		
Upper San Juan	1,800	18	*	V	*	*
Group Campground						
Falcon Group	3,300	3	*	V		*

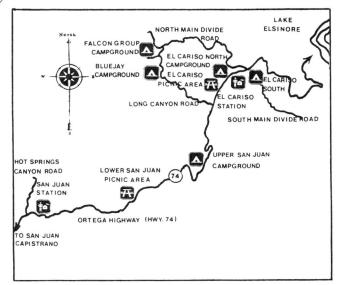

Notes:

Falcon Group Campground has 3 sites: Sage (30 person max.) can take vehicles up to 40 feet; Lupine (40 person max.) has limited parking, primarily for tent camping but can take vehicles up to 20 feet; Yarrow (70 person max.) has limited parking, primarily for tent camping but can take vehicles up to 30 feet; reservations required for all 3 group camps through Mistix.

El Cariso North and Tenaja are open year-round; others are open seasonally.

*Tenaja Campground is located 12 miles west of Murrieta via dirt road in the southeast portion of the Trabuco Ranger District, and is not shown on the map displaying the other campgrounds.

For Information

Trabuco Ranger District
1147 East Sixth Street
Corona, CA 91719
(714) 736-1811

Camping areas get filled fast in the summer, so it's a good idea to call ahead.

REGION 6

Cleveland National Forest *(continued)*

Palomar Ranger District

Campgrounds	Elevation (ft)	# of Units	Drinking Water	Toilets	Trailer Space	Fee Area
Dripping Springs	1,600	25	*	V	*	*
Fry Creek	4,900	20	*	V		*
Indian Flats	3,600	17	*	V		*
Oak Grove	2,800	93	*	F	*	*
Observatory	4,800	42	*	V	*	*
Group Campgrounds						
Crestline Group	4,800	1	*	V		*
Indian Flats Group	3,600	2	*	V		*

Notes:

Crestline Group Campground has 1 unit for 50 persons max.; Indian Flats Group Campground has 2 units for 25 persons each max.; reservations required through Mistix.

Dripping Springs, Oak Grove, and Indian Flats Campgrounds are open all year; the other 3 campgrounds are open May—Nov.

For Information

Palomar Ranger District
1634 Black Canyon Road
Ramona, CA 92065
(619) 788-0250

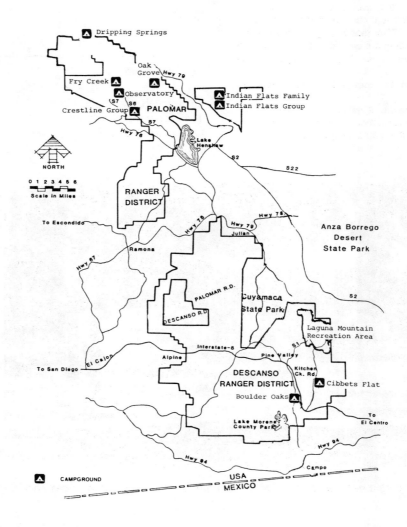

Cleveland National Forest *(continued)*

Descanso Ranger District

Campgrounds	Elevation (ft)	# of Units	Drinking Water	Toilets	Trailer Space	Fee Area
Burnt Rancheria	6,000	108	*	V	*	*
Boulder Oaks	2,800	30	*	V	*	
Cibbets Flat	4,100	23	*	V	*	
Laguna	5,500	105	*	V	*	*
Yerba Santa		32	*	V		*
Group Campgrounds						
Agua Dulce Walk-In		2	*	V		*
El Prado Group		4	*	V	*	*
Horse Heaven Group		3	*	V	*	*
Wooded Hill Group		1	*	V	*	*
Yerba Santa		1	*	V		*

Notes:

Reservations are required for all group campgrounds through Mistix, starting March 1 each year.

Agua Dulce Walk-In has 2 units for 25 and 50 max.; El Prado Group has 4 units each for 30, 40, 50, and 100 max.; Horse Heaven Group has 3 units each for 40, 70, and 100 max.; Wooded Hill Group Camp has 1 group site for 100 max.; and Yerba Santa has 4 tent pads to accommodate 24–32 for all pads.

Yerba Santa Campground is wheelchair accessible and may be used for individuals (6–8/tent pad) or as a group camp.

3 campgrounds are open year-round: Laguna, Cibbets Flat, and Boulder Oaks.

For Information

Descanso Ranger District
3348 Alpine Blvd.
Alpine, CA 92001
(619) 445-6235

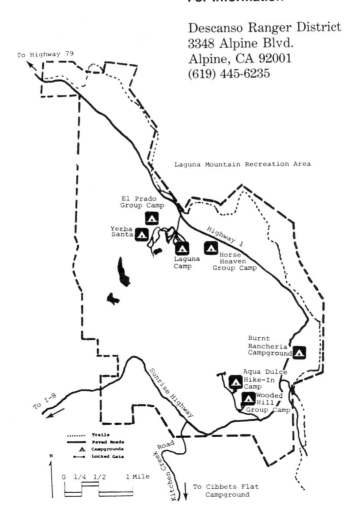

REGION 6

Cuyamaca Rancho State Park

Almost 300 species of birds have been observed in the rugged, mountainous terrain of Cuyamaca Rancho State Park.

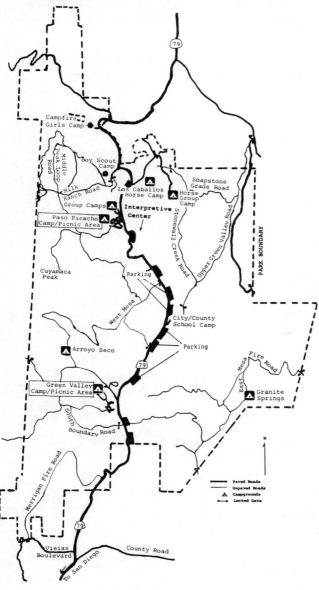

For Information

Cuyamaca Rancho State Park
12551 Highway 79
Descanso, CA 91916
(619) 767-5311

Location

Cuyamaca Rancho State Park is located 9 miles north of I-8 on Highway 79. The park offers beautiful pine and oak forests, broad meadows, and little streams. Nearly 13,000 of the park's 24,677 acres is classified as "wilderness" so all vehicles, even bicycles, are prohibited. The park is in the Peninsular Range of mountains. Park headquarters and most of the campgrounds are at an elevation over 4,000 feet. Cuyamaca Peak, the second highest point in San Diego County, stands at 6,512 feet.

Facilities & Activities

2 developed campgrounds: Paso Picacho and
  Green Valley
85 developed campsites at Paso Picacho
  Campground
  showers
  campsites for disabled
  24-foot trailers; 30-foot campers/motorhomes
  trailer sanitation station
81 developed campsites at Green Valley
  Campground
  showers
  campsites for disabled
  27-foot trailers; 30-foot campers/motorhomes

Cuyamaca Rancho State Park *(continued)*

both campgrounds on State Park Reservation System (all year)

2 group camps at Paso Picacho (A & B)—on State Park Reservation System (mid-April—Oct.); each with 60 person/20 vehicle max.; may be reserved together for 120; developed; showers; wheelchair accessible; no RVs as parking is limited

environmental campsites near Paso Picacho family campground; pit toilet; take own drinking water; short hike

16 developed family equestrian campsites at Los Caballos Campground

    showers

    24-foot trailers; 30-foot campers/motorhomes

    limit 4 horses/site; 2 metal corrals/site; water troughs; trailer in

    on State Park Reservation System (mid-May—Oct.)

primitive trail camps at Arroyo Seco and Granite Springs

    3 family sites up to 8; 1 group site up to 16 at each camp

    pit toilets

    horse corrals available; grazing not allowed; pack in feed

developed group equestrian camp at Los Vaqueros Campground

    showers

    80 person/50 vehicle/45 horse max.

    27-foot trailers; 24-foot motorhomes

    45 metal corrals; water available; trailer in

    on State Park Reservation System (mid-May—Oct.)

picnicking

group picnicking area at Paso Picacho (75 max.)

fishing

hiking and horseback riding trails (over 100 miles)

nature trails

exhibits

Special Notes

The popular 3.5-mile Cuyamaca Peak Trail, from Paso Picacho Campground, is a moderately difficult trail that climbs to the summit for a spectacular view of the ocean, the desert, Mexico, and the Salton Sea. The exhibit at the Stonewall Mine site offers a pictorial history of the greatest of Southern California's gold mines. At the park's interpretive center at Paso Picacho are exhibits on the plants and animals of the region, and the museum at the park headquarters tells the story of the native people who lived here for centuries.

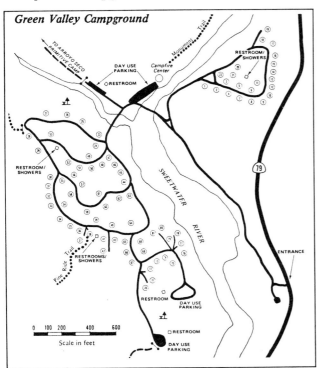

Green Valley Campground

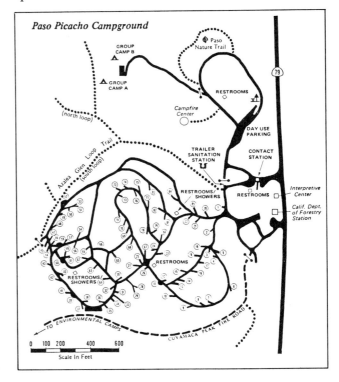

Paso Picacho Campground

REGION 6

Joshua Tree National Monument

For Information

Superintendent
Joshua Tree National Monument
74485 National Monument Drive
Twentynine Palms, CA 92277-3597
(619) 367-7511

Location

Joshua Tree National Monument is located 140 miles east of Los Angeles. From the west it is approached via I-10 (U.S. 60) and Twentynine Palms Highway (SH 62) to the north entrances at the town of Joshua Tree or Twentynine Palms. The Cottonwood Spring, or south entrance, is 25 miles east of Indio via I-10. The 559,954-acre park is rich in ecological, historical, and recreational resources. It has 467,000 acres designated as wilderness.

Special Notes

Two deserts come together at Joshua Tree National Monument. Few areas more vividly illustrate the contrast between high and low desert. Below 3,000 feet, the Colorado Desert, occupying the eastern half of the monument, is dominated by the abundant creosote bush. The higher, slightly cooler, and wetter Mojave Desert in the western half of the monument is the special habitat of the undisciplined Joshua tree. Five fan-palm oases dot the monument, indicating those few areas where water occurs naturally at or near the surface.

Average minimum temperatures at Twentynine Palms Oasis (at an elevation of 1,960 feet) in December through February are in the 30s; at higher elevations, temperatures will average approximately eleven degrees lower. The number of days with 100° or higher varies from 62–101 days per year with an average of 80.7 days per year. Hundred-degree temperatures have been recorded as early as April 18 and as late as October 19. The park enjoys an average of 259 clear days per year.

All of the campgrounds are located between 3,000–4,500 feet elevation and many of them are

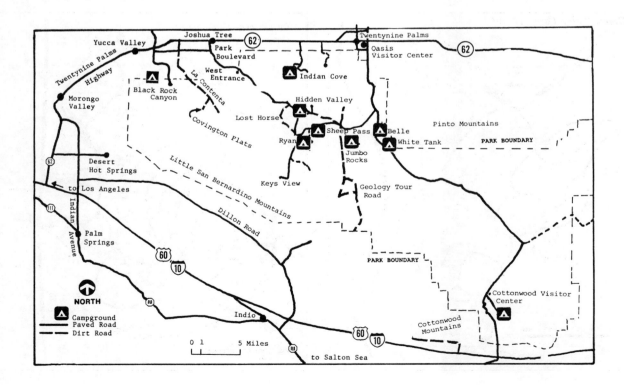

tucked in and around the unique boulder clusters that crown the central area. During the summer months, the lower elevations such as Pinto Basin are rather harsh environments in which to hike. However, the upper elevations provide enjoyable walking conditions year round, especially in the Covington area.

The temperatures around Joshua Tree National Monument exceed 100°F for about 80 days per year, but the nights are cool, as are the days at higher elevations.

Facilities & Activities

9 campgrounds, with 535 campsites (see chart) first-come, first-served basis; no reservations tables, fireplaces, toilets
(*Note*: some are closed each summer)
3 group campgrounds; reservations required; not open in summer
campers must bring their own water and firewood or fuel; if you run out of water, it can be obtained at either the Twentynine Palms Visitor Center, Indian Cove Ranger Station, or at Cottonwood Campground
backcountry camping; permit required; no fee
picnicking (developed sites at Indian Cove and Cottonwood; undeveloped sites throughout park)
18-mile self-guiding motor nature tour
9 self-guiding interpretive trails
hiking trails (information sheet available)
cross-country hiking and backpacking
horseback riding

horses allowed at Ryan and Black Rock Campgrounds; riders must provide feed and water
35 miles of the California Riding and Hiking Trail pass through the park
no motor vehicles are permitted off established roads
ranger-conducted activities on week-ends during fall and spring
wayside exhibits
3 visitor centers

	Total sites	RVs	Tents	Fee	Limit of stay	Drinking water	Flush toilets	Sanitary dump	Camp store
Tent/RV Campgrounds									
Belle	20	●	●		14				
Black Rock (horse camping only)	ltd	●	●	●	14	●	●	●	
Cottonwood	62	●	●	●	14	●	●		
Hidden Valley	62	●	●		14				
Indian Cove	114	●	●		14				
Jumbo Rocks	130	●	●		14				
Ryan	27	●	●		14				
White Tank	20	●	●		14				
Group Campgrounds									
Cottonwood (walk-in)	3		●	●	14	●	●		
Indian Cove (walk-in)	13		●	●	14				
Sheep Pass (walk-in)	6		●	●	14				
Backcountry Campsites									
Various locations (hike-in)	open		●						

REGION 6

Lake Elsinore State Recreation Area

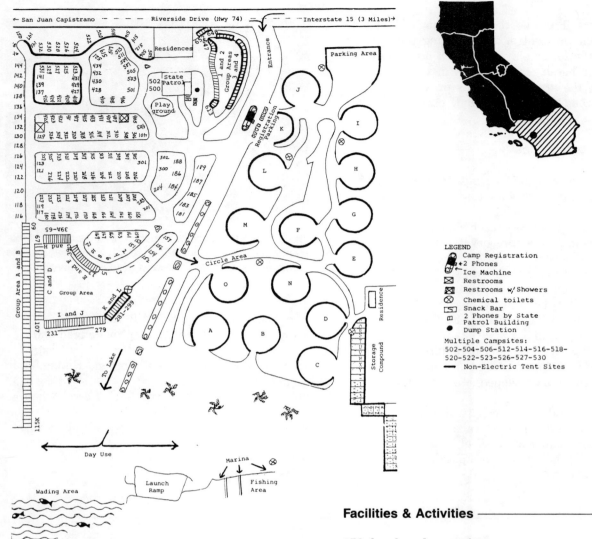

LEGEND
- Camp Registration
- 2 Phones
- Ice Machine
- ⊠ Restrooms
- ⊠ Restrooms w/ Showers
- ⊗ Chemical toilets
- Snack Bar
- 2 Phones by State Patrol Building
- ● Dump Station

Multiple Campsites:
502-504-506-512-514-516-518-
520-522-523-526-527-530
— Non-Electric Tent Sites

For Information

Lake Elsinore State Recreation Area
17801 Lake Perris Drive
Perris, CA 92370
(714) 674-3005

Location

Lake Elsinore State Recreation Area is located 22 miles southeast of Corona via SH 71 and SH 74 on the north end of Lake Elsinore. Located in Riverside County, the 2,954-acre park has an elevation of 1,234 feet.

Facilities & Activities

176 developed campsites
132 of the developed sites have electrical hookups
campsites for disabled
28-foot trailers; 31-foot campers/motorhomes
group camping area (350 persons/100 vehicle max.)
picnicking
group picnicking area (350 max.)
fishing
swimming
boating (launch ramp, rentals, water skiing)
food service

Special Notes

Lake Elsinore, nestled in a little valley between mountain ridges, offers a variety of water sports. Bicyclists also enjoy touring the area.

Lake Perris State Recreation Area

For Information

Lake Perris State Recreation Area
17801 Lake Perris Drive
Perris, CA 92370
(714) 675-0676

Location

Lake Perris State Recreation Area is located 11 miles southeast of Riverside via Moreno Beach Drive from U.S. 60 or via Lake Perris Drive and Ramona Expressway from I-215. In Riverside County, the 8,000-acre recreation area has an elevation of 1,575 feet.

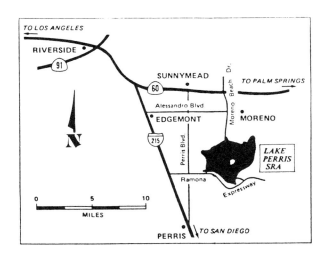

Facilities & Activities

167 developed campsites for tents
264 hookup sites (water, electricity, sink disposal)
campsites for disabled
showers
31-foot trailers; 31-foot campers/motorhomes
trailer sanitation station near entrance
6 group campground areas (each accommodates from 25–100 people; developed; showers)
3 group campground areas at Bernasconi (each accommodates from 25–80 people; chemical toilets; no showers)
picnicking
6 group picnicking areas (100 max., each site)
1 group picnicking area at Bernasconi (25–100)
fishing
hiking trail
swimming
exhibits
horseback riding trail

On the winding, narrow roads in California parks, always be prepared for someone coming around the next turn.

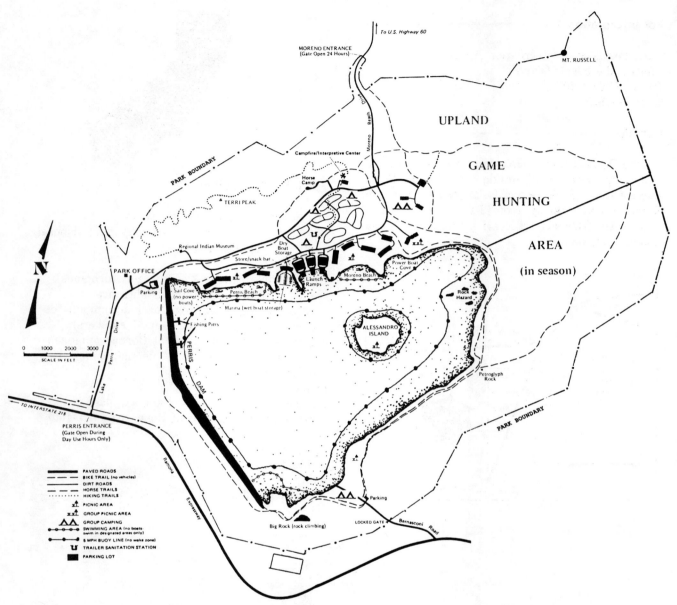

To U.S. Highway 60

MORENO ENTRANCE
(Gate Open 24 Hours)

MT. RUSSELL

UPLAND

GAME

HUNTING

AREA

(in season)

PARK BOUNDARY

Campfire/Interpretive Center

Horse
Camp

TERRI PEAK

Regional Indian Museum

PARK OFFICE

Parking

Dry
Boat
Storage

Store/snack bar

Power Boat
Cove

Moreno Beach

Sail Cove
(no power
boats)

Perris Beach

Launch
Ramps

Rock
Hazard

Marina (wet boat storage)

Fishing Piers

ALESSANDRO
ISLAND

PERRIS DAM

Petroglyph
Rock

TO INTERSTATE 215

PERRIS ENTRANCE
(Gate Open During
Day Use Hours Only)

PARK BOUNDARY

N

0   1000   2000   3000
SCALE IN FEET

Ramona Expressway

Lake Perris Drive

Moreno Beach Drive

Legend:
- PAVED ROADS
- BIKE TRAIL (no vehicles)
- DIRT ROADS
- HORSE TRAILS
- HIKING TRAILS
- PICNIC AREA
- GROUP PICNIC AREA
- GROUP CAMPING
- SWIMMING AREA (no boats-swim in designated areas only)
- 5 MPH BUOY LINE (no wake zone)
- TRAILER SANITATION STATION
- PARKING LOT

Big Rock (rock climbing)

LOCKED GATE

Bernasconi Road

Parking

equestrian camping (50 horse/rider max.; 6 metal corrals; water troughs; trailer in)
boating (launch ramp, mooring, rentals, water skiing, gas dock, boat supplies)
food service
designated underwater area
on State Park Reservation System (April—Sept.)

Special Notes

Formed by Perris Dam, the lake offers water sports and a special SCUBA diving area. Thousands of acres of rugged surrounding land are open to hiking, and in a special area just south of the dam, rock climbing. Climbers may park at the Bernasconi area and take the bicycle trail to Big Rock for a variety of challenges and many spectacular views. A map of the Big Rock area is available at the kiosks.

Alessandro Island, a day use boat-in only area, has picnic tables under shade ramadas; grills are nearby. There's a trail leading to the top of the island where fine views of the area can be enjoyed. A 9-mile hiking and bicycling trail encircles the lake. It is paved except for a short stretch at the south end of the dam. A horse trail circles the lake and goes on into the undeveloped part of the recreation area.

Leo Carillo State Beach

For Information

Leo Carillo State Beach
1925 Las Virgenes
Calabasas, CA 91302
(818) 880-0350
1-800-533-7275

Location

Leo Carillo State Beach is located in Los Angeles County, 28 miles west of Santa Monica on Highway 1. The 1,602-acre park is famous for its 6,600-foot beach and more than 1,000 acres of upland, where elevations reach 1,500 feet.

fishing
hiking trail
swimming
nature trail
supplies
on State Park Reservation System (March—Nov.)

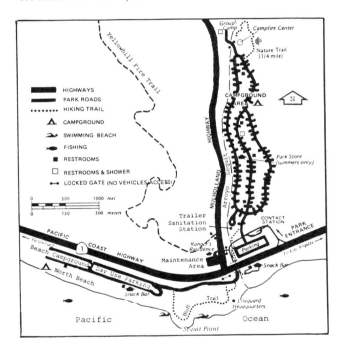

Special Notes

The beach is divided into 2 separate areas by Sequit Point, a bluff riddled with caves and a sea-carved tunnel. Each area has a snack bar, beach equipment rental, and restroom facility with dressing rooms. Summer ocean temperatures here are usually in the high 60s; good surfing and skin diving. Hikers should watch for poison oak as the plant is plentiful in the park.

Facilities & Activities

2 campgrounds
138 developed campsites in canyon
50 developed campsites at beach (25 tent sites; 25 trailer sites); accessible only to vehicles less than 8 feet in height
campsites for disabled
showers
31-foot trailers; 31-foot campers/motorhomes
trailer sanitation station
group camping area (50 person/18 vehicle max.; 100-yard walk-in; showers; tent camping only; no camping in parking lot)

Leo Carillo State Beach is a popular camping area because of its excellent opportunities for water sports.

McGrath State Beach

For Information

McGrath State Beach
24 East Main Street
Ventura, CA 93001
(805) 654-4744

Location

McGrath State Beach is located in Ventura. Visitors southbound on U.S. 101 should take the Seaward Avenue off-ramp to Harbor Boulevard, turn left on Harbor and go 3 miles to the park. Northbound visitors on U.S. 101 take the Victoria Avenue exit, left at the signal to Olivas Park Drive, then right to Harbor Boulevard. Turn left on Harbor and go ¾-mile to the park. The 295-acre state beach is located in Ventura County.

Facilities & Activities

174 developed campsites
campsites for disabled
showers
30-foot trailers; 34-foot campers/motorhomes
trailer sanitation station
fishing
swimming
nature trail
on State Park Reservation System (all year)

Special Notes

McGrath State Beach stretches from the Santa Clara River near Oxnard south for 2 miles along the Pacific Ocean. Lifeguards are on duty in the summer, but swimming is not recommended because of the strong currents. A row of sand dunes overlooks the surf between the campsites and the beach. The northern half of McGrath State Beach contains the

Even if you're camping in a "tent on wheels," the important thing is to get out and enjoy what California parks have to offer.

160-acre Santa Clara Estuary Natural Preserve. A ½-mile self-guided trail winds through a portion of the preserve.

Emma Wood State Beach Group Camp is operated by the state (Channel Coast District), while Ventura County operates *Emma Wood Beach Park*.

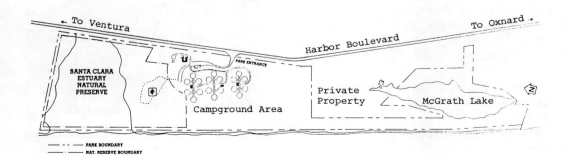

McGrath State Beach (continued)

Emma Wood Beach is located 4 miles north of Ventura on U.S. 101 and has 116 acres. Called Ventura River, there are 4 group camps; each with 30 person/5 vehicle max.; outside cold showers; tent camping only; may be reserved together for a group up to 120 persons with maximum 20 vehicles. Very limited parking. No RVs or buses; on State Park Reservation System (all year).

For information, phone (805) 643-7532.

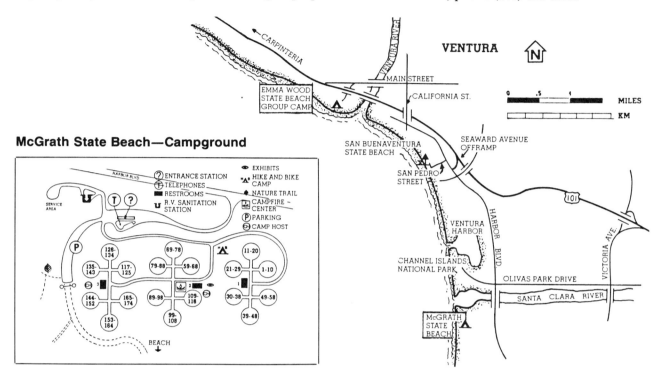

Be careful about rushing into the surf of an unfamiliar beach—there may be strong currents (see page 138).

Mount San Jacinto State Park and Wilderness

For Information

Mount San Jacinto State Wilderness
17801 Lake Perris Drive
Perris, CA 92370
(714) 659-2607

United States Forest Service
San Jacinto Ranger District
P.O. Box 518
(54270 Pinecrest Ave.)
Idyllwild, CA 92549
(714) 659-2117

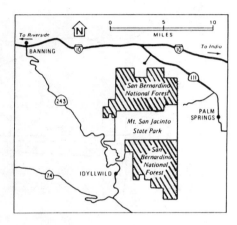

Location

Mount San Jacinto State Park, in Riverside County, is on Highway 243 near Idyllwild. The 3,482-acre park, with an elevation of 5,500 feet is adjacent to the Mount San Jacinto State Wilderness. Access to the 10,040-acre Wilderness area is from Highway 243 near Idyllwild or by tram from Palm Springs.

Facilities & Activities

33 developed campsites at Idyllwild Campground
  showers
50 primitive campsites at Stone Creek
  Campground
  no showers
both campgrounds on State Park Reservation
  System (May—Sept.)
(see chart on 4 other campgrounds operated by
  U.S. Forest Service)

group campground at Black Mountain Group
  Camp, operated by the U.S. Forest Service;
  accommodates 2 groups of 50; parking for 16
  vehicles; no trailers/motorhomes; pit toilets;
  water
4 designated hike-in campsites in the state
  wilderness; permit required; no more than 15
  people in a group
picnicking
nature trail
hiking trails
horseback riding trails
equestrian camping (max. of 15 horses/riders)

Special Notes

This is true primitive high-country wilderness area with granite peaks, forests, and fern-bordered mountain meadows. Mount San Jacinto is only one of 5 peaks in California higher than 10,000 feet. A popular attraction is the breathtaking Palm Springs Aerial Tramway, a 2.5-mile ride that rises from 2,643 feet at the Valley Station to 8,516 feet at the Mountain Station on the edge of the wilderness. The tram operates every day, all year long, except for approximately 4 weeks after Labor Day.

The San Jacinto Wilderness is operated by 2 agencies: The California Department of Parks and Recreation administers Mount San Jacinto State Wilderness; the U.S. Forest Service operates San Bernardino National Forest Wilderness. Rules for the use of the 2 areas are generally the same but there are important differences. Wilderness users should be aware of the rules governing the area they are in. They should obtain a hiking map of the San Jacinto Wilderness that clearly states the regulations. Wilderness permits are required for entering the wilderness, whether for a day-trip or an overnight trip.

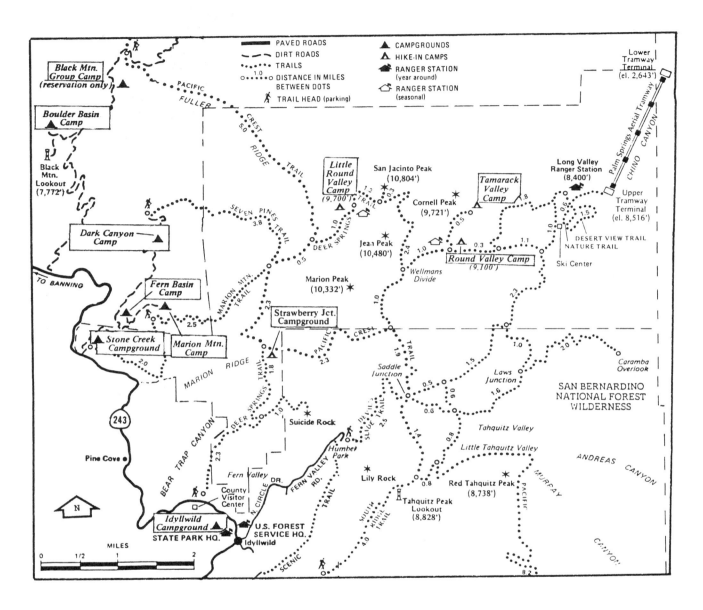

Campgrounds	Elevation (ft)	# of Units	Trailers/Campers	Toilets
Idyllwild	5,300	33	24/24	F
Stone Creek	5,900	50	24/24	P
Marion Mountain	6,400	26	18/	P
Dark Canyon	5,800	22	None	P
Boulder Basin	7,300	34	18/	P
Fern Basin	6,300	24	18/	P

If you are camping, you must get your permit from the agency that administers the area where you plan to spend the night. Overnight permits for either agency are honored for travel through the other agency's lands, and day-use permits issued by either agency are honored by both.

You must get a permit for day use in person on the day of your trip, at one of the two ranger stations in Idyllwild. You can get a camping permit in advance only by mail. If they are still available, you can also get a camping permit on the day of your trip.

REGION 6

Ocotillo Wells State Vehicular Recreation Area

For Information

Ocotillo Wells State Vehicular Recreation Area
P.O. Box 356
Borrego Springs, CA 92004
(619) 767-5391

Location

Ocotillo Wells State Vehicular Recreation Area is located on SH 78 at Ocotillo Wells. The 14,532-acre recreation area is in San Diego County and borders Anza-Borrego Desert State Park to the north and west. The elevation is 100 feet.

Facilities & Activities

no official campground
entire off-road area is available for camping
chemical toilets
no camping fee/no day-use fee
plenty of level area for tent and motorhome camping
no water

Special Notes

Virtually the entire area is open to off-road vehicular recreation. Open daily, 24 hours for motorcycles, 4-wheel drive, all-terrain vehicles, and dune buggies. This park offers desert terrain for off-highway vehicles. The sights at dawn and dusk provide vistas of spectacular natural beauty.

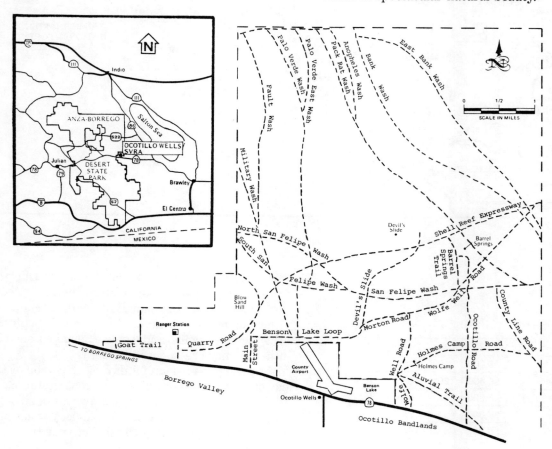

Orange County State Beaches

The beaches in Orange County reach from Seal Beach, down coast of Long Beach, to San Clemente. This section of coast ranges from broad sandy beaches backed by low-lying plains and wetlands to high cliffs and sandy coves. This pleasant environment provides opportunities for swimming, sunbathing, boating, fishing, diving, and surfing. Three of the state beaches located in Orange County have camping facilities: namely, Bolsa Chica, Doheny, and San Clemente.

You can have a great time on California beaches and never get your feet wet.

REGION 6

Bolsa Chica State Beach

For Information

Bolsa Chica State Beach
18331 Enterprise Lane
Huntington Beach, CA 92648
(714) 846-3460

Location

The 164-acre, Bolsa Chica State Beach is located 3 miles up coast of Huntington Beach on Highway 1. The beach is 6 miles long but only the northern 3 miles are developed with facilities. The southern end has steep cliffs between the road and beach with several accessways. A bike path/walkway extends the entire length of the beach.

Facilities & Activities

50 enroute campsites for self-contained RVs
accommodations for disabled
cold showers
no reservations; first-come, first-served
picnicking
fishing
swimming
food service

Doheny State Beach

For Information

Doheny State Beach
25300 Harbor Drive
Dana Point, CA 92629
(714) 496-6172

Location

The 62-acre Doheny State Beach is at the south end of Dana Point near the intersection of I-5 and Highway 1. The southern area of this park is for camping and the northern area is for day use. The day-use area features a 5-acre lawn surrounded by extensive picnic facilities. Surfing is popular, but restricted to the north end of the beach.

Facilities & Activities

120 developed campsites
showers
24-foot trailers; 28-foot campers/motorhomes
trailer sanitation station
on State Park Reservation System (all year)
picnicking
group picnicking area (500 max.)
fishing
swimming
exhibits
food service
supplies
designated underwater area

As the 17th century angler Isaac Walton observed, "Angling may be said to be so like the mathematics that it can never be fully learnt," and add a 20th century remark, "practice makes perfect."

San Clemente State Beach

For Information

San Clemente State Beach
3030 Avenida Del Presidente
San Clemente, CA 92672
(714) 492-3156

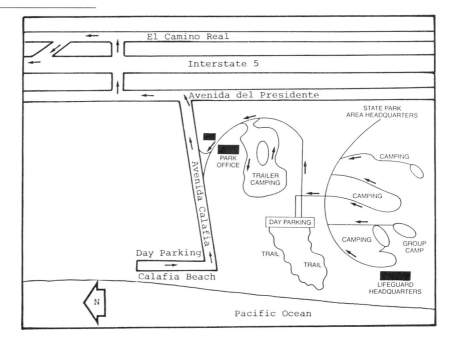

Location

The 110-acre San Clemente State Beach is at the south end of San Clemente on I-5. Surfing is popular on the north end of the 1-mile beach. Elevation is 100 feet above sea level.

Facilities & Activities

85 developed campsites
campsites for disabled
24-foot trailers; 28-foot campers/motorhomes
72 full-hookup campsites for 30-foot vehicles
showers
group camping area (50 person/16 vehicle
    max.)—on State Park Reservation System (all
    year); developed; showers; 30-foot max.
picnicking
fishing
hiking trail
swimming
on State Park Reservation System (all year)

It's really not as difficult as it looks to get to San Clemente State Beach.

REGION 6

Palomar Mountain State Park

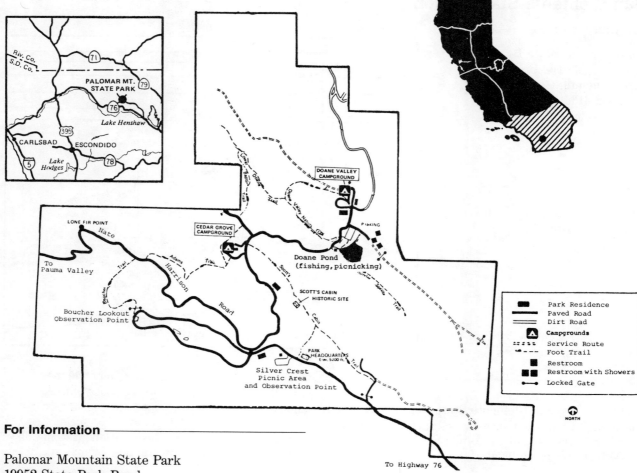

For Information

Palomar Mountain State Park
19952 State Park Road
Palomar Mountain, CA 92060
(619) 742-3462

Location

Palomar Mountain State Park is located in San Diego County near the world-famous Palomar Observatory. From SH 76 either of 2 roads can be used to reach the park. The one from Rincon Springs is scenic but rather steep and winding. County Road S7 from Lake Henshaw is longer, but its gentle grade makes it more suitable for heavily loaded vehicles and those pulling trailers. The 1,897-acre park has an average elevation of 5,500 feet.

Facilities & Activities

31 developed campsites at Doane Valley
    campsites for disabled
    showers
    21-foot trailers; 21-foot campers/motorhomes

3 group camps at Cedar Grove (one 25 person/8
    vehicle camp; two 15 person/5 vehicle camps; or
    any combination up to 55 persons; developed;
    showers)
picnicking
fishing
hiking trails
nature trails
on State Park Reservation System (all year)

Special Notes

Large pine, fir, and cedar trees make the park one of the few areas in southern California with a Sierra Nevada-like atmosphere. Summer evenings are cool and from several places you can look out over large areas of southern California ocean and desert. Doane Pond is stocked with trout and fishing is especially good during the winter, spring and early summer.

Picacho State Recreation Area

For Information

Picacho State Recreation Area
P.O. Box 3166
North Shore, CA 92254
(619) 393-3059

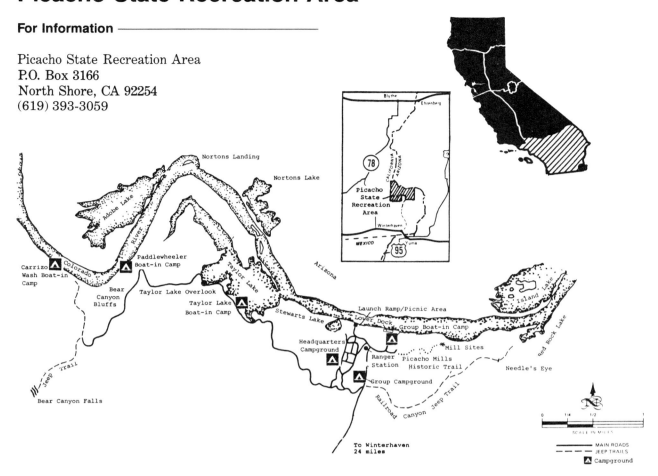

Location

Picacho State Recreation Area is located in the lower Colorado River Basin, 25 miles north of Winterhaven. The first 5 miles of the road from I-8 (just east of Winterhaven) are paved, but the next 18 miles are rough and unpaved. This 4,880-acre park is in Imperial County at 190 feet elevation.

Facilities & Activities

50 primitive campsites
solar showers
24-foot trailers; 30-foot campers/motorhomes
2 group camping areas: 1 for boat-in, 1 for
   drive-in
picnicking
fishing
hiking trails
exhibits
boating (launch ramp, rentals, water skiing,
   boat-in-camp, on board camping)

Special Notes

The most popular attraction at Picacho is the cool, green Colorado River. Whether it's for fishing, boating, or sightseeing, it's a pleasant sight to behold. The level of the river is sometimes high and sometimes low depending on how much water is released from the dam upriver. Fifty-five miles of open river and many backwater lakes are accessible from the recreation area as Parker Dam is 40 miles upstream and Imperial Dam is 15 miles downstream.

The autumn and early spring months are the most popular time to float down the river. The best times to visit are between October and April as mosquitos are a problem from April on into mid-summer. Offering gorgeous desert scenery along the lower Colorado River Basin, the area is dominated by Picacho Peak, a plug-dome volcanic outcropping. Campers should come prepared, as the nearest phone, grocery store, bait, dump station, etc. is 27 miles away.

Point Mugu State Park

For Information

Point Mugu State Park
1925 Las Virgenes
Calabasas, CA 91302
(818) 880-0350
1-800-533-7275

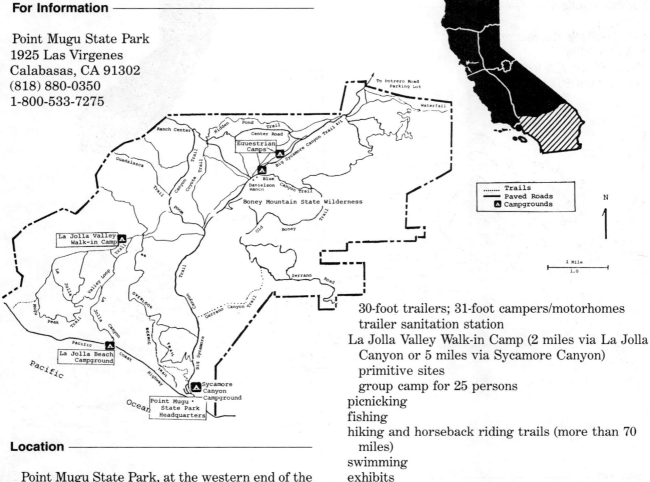

Location

Point Mugu State Park, at the western end of the Santa Monica Mountains in Ventura County, is located 15 miles south of Oxnard on Highway 1. This 14,980-acre park has some 5 miles of ocean shoreline, with rocky bluffs, sandy beaches, a spectacular sand dune, rugged hills and uplands, 2 major canyons, and wide grassy valleys dotted with sycamores, oaks, and a few native walnuts.

Facilities & Activities

2 campgrounds: Big Sycamore Canyon and La Jolla Beach
50 developed campsites at Big Sycamore Canyon Campground
  showers
  campsites for disabled
  31-foot trailers; 31-foot campers/motorhomes
  special campsites for hikers/bicyclists
100 primitive campsites at La Jolla Beach Campground
  no showers

30-foot trailers; 31-foot campers/motorhomes
  trailer sanitation station
La Jolla Valley Walk-in Camp (2 miles via La Jolla Canyon or 5 miles via Sycamore Canyon)
  primitive sites
  group camp for 25 persons
picnicking
fishing
hiking and horseback riding trails (more than 70 miles)
swimming
exhibits
2 equestrian camping areas: Sycamore and Danielson multi-use areas
  At Danielson: minimum of 10 horses, maximum of 75
  At Sycamore: minimum of 10 horses, maximum of 40
  access only via Newbury Park; trailer in; water troughs
Sycamore Canyon and La Jolla Beach Campgrounds both on State Park Reservation System (March—Nov.)

Special Notes

The park's name comes from "muwu," a word meaning "beach" in the language of the Chumash Indians. They had lived here for more than 6,000 years when Spanish explorer Juan Cabrillo dropped anchor off this coast in October, 1542. The park's sandy beaches provide good swimming, body surfing, beachcombing, and surf fishing.

Providence Mountains State Recreation Area

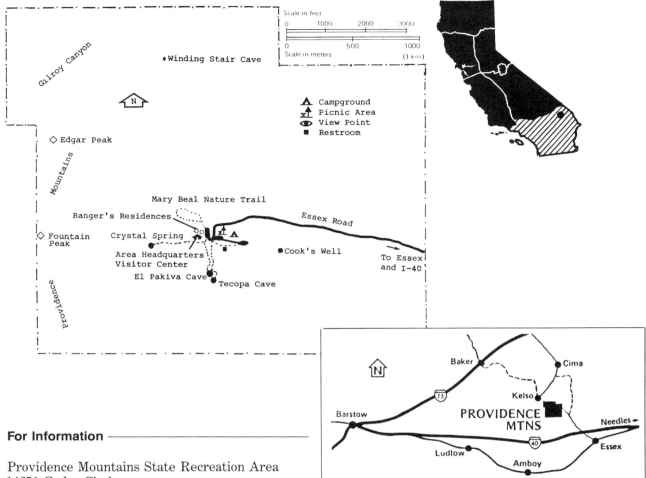

For Information

Providence Mountains State Recreation Area
14651 Cedar Circle
Hesperia, CA 92345
(619) 389-2281

Location

Providence Mountains State Recreation Area is located 17 miles northwest of I-40 near Essex on Essex Road. This 5,250-acre recreation area is in San Bernardino County about 80 air miles east of Barstow in the center of the eastern Mojave Desert. Park headquarters at 4,300 feet elevation overlooks some three hundred square miles of desert valleys and mountains.

Facilities & Activities

6 primitive campsites
no showers
31-foot trailers; 32-foot campers/motorhomes
nature trail
exhibits

Special Notes

This recreation area features Mitchell Caverns Natural Preserve, where El Pakiva and Tecopa Caverns, filled with intricate limestone formations, are open to the public. The area is *closed in the summer*. From September 16 through June 15 tours are conducted at 1:30 p.m. on weekdays and at 10:00 a.m., 1:30 p.m. and 3:00 p.m. on weekends and holidays. Due in large part to the elevation, temperatures in the park are usually moderate the year-round, though the months from October to May are most favored by visitors. The caverns remain at a nearly constant 65°F.

When you visit bring water (park supplies are very limited), as well as extra food and gasoline as a normal precaution when traveling in the desert. This sunscorched land of broad valleys is filled with cactus, creosote bush, sand dunes, cinder cones, and dramatic piñon-clad mountain ranges in the eastern Mojave Desert.

REGION 6

Saddleback Butte State Park

For Information

Saddleback Butte State Park
17102 East Avenue "J" East
Lancaster, CA 93535
(805) 942-0662

Location

Saddleback Butte State Park is located 17 miles east of Lancaster on Avenue J East on the western edge of the Mojave Desert. The 2,875-acre park surrounds the 3,651-foot Saddleback Butte, a granite mountain top that stands some one thousand feet above the broad alluvial bottomland of the Antelope Valley. The Los Angeles County state park was established in 1960 to protect the butte as well as to preserve a representative example of the native Joshua-tree woodland.

Facilities & Activities

50 primitive campsites
campsites for disabled
no showers
pit toilets
30-foot trailers; 30-foot campers/motorhomes
trailer sanitation station

Joshua Tree Group Campground (30 person/12 vehicle max.)—on State Park Reservation System; all year; primitive; no showers; limit 2 RVs; no trailers; very limited parking
picnicking
hiking trail
nature trail
exhibits

Special Notes

The best time to visit this park is in the springtime (February through May) when wildflowers are apt to put on a fine display of color. Autumn (October and November) is also likely to be pleasant. Summer temperatures average 95°F but occasionally range on up to as much as 115°F.

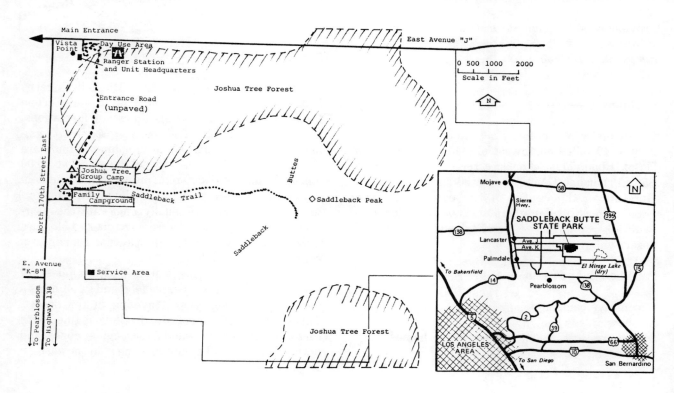

Salton Sea State Recreation Area

For Information

Salton Sea State Recreation Area
P.O. Box 3166
North Shore, CA 92254
(619) 393-3059

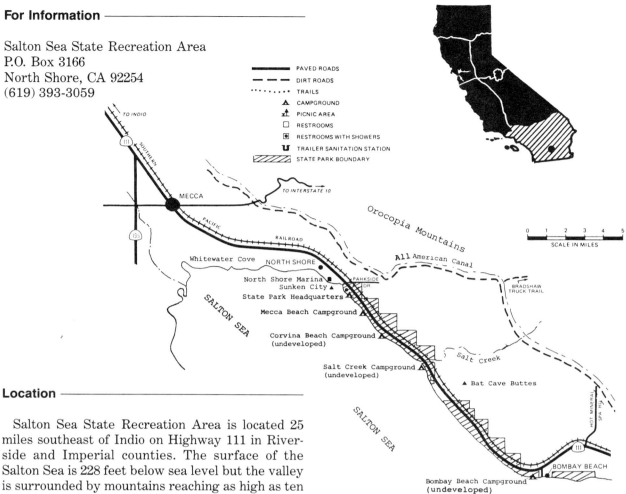

LEGEND:
PAVED ROADS
DIRT ROADS
TRAILS
▲ CAMPGROUND
⬥ PICNIC AREA
□ RESTROOMS
▣ RESTROOMS WITH SHOWERS
U TRAILER SANITATION STATION
STATE PARK BOUNDARY

Location

Salton Sea State Recreation Area is located 25 miles southeast of Indio on Highway 111 in Riverside and Imperial counties. The surface of the Salton Sea is 228 feet below sea level but the valley is surrounded by mountains reaching as high as ten thousand feet. The 17,900-acre recreation area is 220 feet below sea level.

Facilities & Activities

5 campgrounds
148 developed campsites (headquarters and Mecca Beach)
15 full hookup sites (headquarters)
campsites for disabled
solar showers (headquarters and Mecca Beach)
30-foot trailers; 35-foot campers/motorhomes
trailer sanitation station
800 primitive sites (Corvina Beach, Salt Creek, and Bombay Beach) with dirt roads, chemical toilets, accommodates largest RVs, sites on the water's edge, pull boats up on the beach to campsite, bring own water to Salt Creek
group camping area (120 person/70 vehicle max.)
picnicking
fishing
swimming
nature trails
exhibits
boating (launch ramp, mooring)
on State Park Reservation System—only Headquarters Campground (mid-Oct.—May)

Special Notes

One of Southern California's most popular boating parks, this is also one of the world's largest inland bodies of salt water. The Salton Sea is about 35 miles long and 15 miles wide at its widest point, with more than 360 square miles of surface and 110 miles of shoreline. It's fairly shallow—average overall depth is less than 20 feet. Water temperatures vary from 55°F in winter to 92°F in summer. Fall and spring are the favorite times to visit the area. The mild temperatures make outdoor activities a pleasure.

San Bernardino National Forest

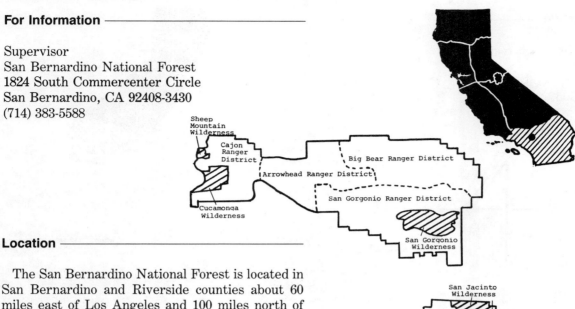

For Information

Supervisor
San Bernardino National Forest
1824 South Commercenter Circle
San Bernardino, CA 92408-3430
(714) 383-5588

Location

The San Bernardino National Forest is located in San Bernardino and Riverside counties about 60 miles east of Los Angeles and 100 miles north of San Diego. The 819,000-acre forest is located in parts of four mountain ranges in Southern California. Part of the forest is in the San Gabriel and the San Bernardino Mountains. The part south of the San Gorgonio Pass occupies the San Jacinto Mountains that grade into the Santa Rosa Mountains.

Special Notes

The San Bernardino National Forest is characterized by steep rugged topography with sharply distinct ridges and draws. Elevations range from 1,000 feet in the front country to 11,502-feet San Gorgonio Peak, the highest peak in Southern California. Vegetation ranges from chaparral to coniferous forests to desert trees.

History buffs will enjoy the historic Gold Fever Trail, a 3-hour self-guided auto tour along 11½ miles of dirt road in the Big Bear Ranger District. Big Bear Lake, with 22 miles of shoreline offers a variety of water sports, but swimming is not allowed. State and county beaches are available at Silverwood, Gregory, Arrowhead, and Green Valley Lakes.

The Pacific Crest National Scenic Trail traverses five of the ranger districts for a distance of 146 miles. There are more than 500 miles of other trails such as self-guided nature trails, hiking, backpacking, and equestrian trails. In fact, equestrians will find numerous riding opportunities in the forest.

Five winter sport sites are located in the forest in the Big Bear and Snow Valley areas east of Lake Arrowhead. Be aware that some Forest Service

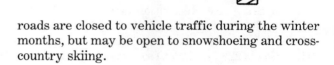

roads are closed to vehicle traffic during the winter months, but may be open to snowshoeing and cross-country skiing.

Wilderness Areas

The San Bernardino National Forest has three Wilderness Areas totally within it and two others are shared with Angeles National Forest. The 20,160-acre *Santa Rosa Wilderness* is located in the southeast sector of the San Jacinto Ranger District. It is a rugged, boulder strewn area with highly eroded canyons and washes, valleys and steep cliffs. Vegetation ranges from desert agave, ocotillo, and cresote to mountain piñon pine and juniper.

The 32,851-acre *San Jacinto Wilderness* lies on either side of the San Jacinto State Park and State Wilderness and has a common trail system. Excellent rockclimbing opportunities exist. There are entry quotas for all travel zones in this heavily used wilderness area.

The *San Gorgonio Wilderness*, in the southeast sector of the forest's north unit, embraces the summit region of the San Bernardino Mountain range, the highest in Southern California. There are 27 ap-

San Bernardino National Forest *(continued)*

proved and designated camping sites (all above 7,100-feet elevation) accessible from 6 different trailheads. A wilderness permit is required, even for day hiking.

The two wilderness areas adjoining the Angeles National Forest are the *Cucamonga Wilderness* and the *Sheep Mountain Wilderness*. More than two-thirds of Cucamonga Wilderness but only a small parcel of Sheep Mountain Wilderness are in the Cajon Ranger District. Access to the wilderness areas is from Lytle Creek Canyon area. Permits are required and Cucamonga is on the quota system for all travel zones. Both areas are quite rugged, with sharp peaks and steep mountainsides.

Cajon Ranger District

Star Route, Box 100
1209 Lytle Creek Canyon Road
Lytle Creek, CA 92359
(714) 887-2576

Camping Facilities

Applewhite Campground, in Lytle Creek Canyon, is the only improved camping facility in the Cajon Ranger District. There are 44 sites; trailers up to 22 feet long can be accommodated; fees are charged; drinking water is available; and there are single as well as multi-family sites. Elevation is 3,300 feet and the campground is open year-round. There are no group camping sites available.

Visitors can camp in remote areas where there are no stoves, tables, or restrooms. It's free but check at the ranger station for dispersed camping permit and campfire rules and regulations.

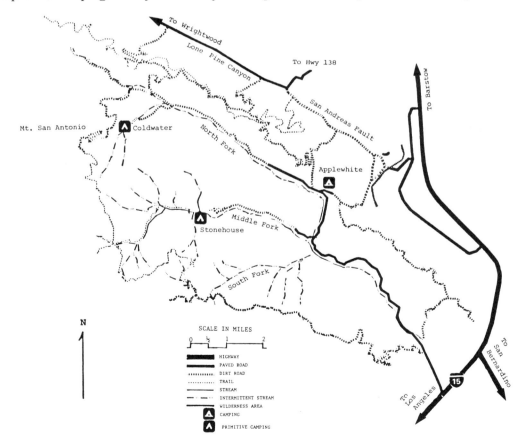

San Bernardino National Forest *(continued)*

Arrowhead Ranger District

Family Campgrounds	Elevation (ft)	People/Vehicle	# of Units	Drinking Water	Trailers	Site Fee
Crab Flats	6,200		29	*	*	*
Dogwood	5,600		93	*	*	*
Green Valley	7,000		36	*	*	*
North Shore	5,300		27	*	*	*
Group Campgrounds						
Fisherman's	5,400	20				
Shady Cove (2)	7,500	25&75/15		*		*
Tent Peg	5,400	25/5				*

Notes:
Dogwood and Green Valley are also multi-family campgrounds.
North Shore is open only on weekends.
Fisherman's is accessible by trail.
Reservations required for all group camps through Arrowhead Ranger District office.

For Information

Arrowhead Ranger District
P.O. Box 7
28104 Highway 18, SkyForest
Rimforest, CA 92378
(714) 337-2444

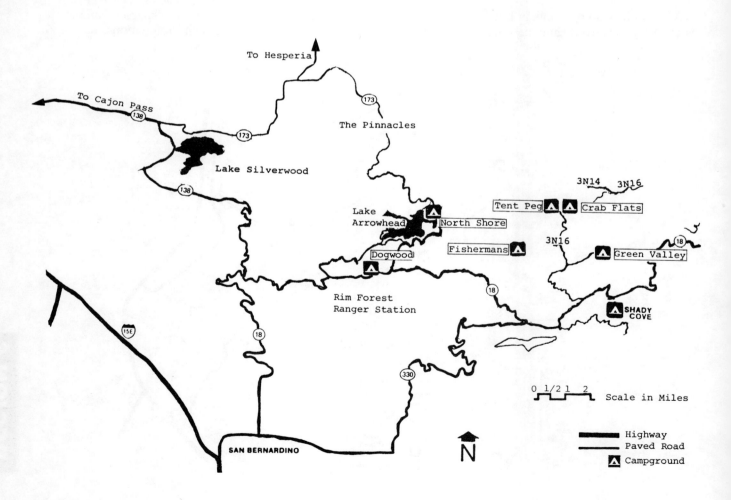

San Bernardino National Forest *(continued)*

Big Bear Ranger District

Family Campgrounds	Elevation (ft)	People/Vehicle	# of Units	Drinking Water	Trailers	Site Fee
Big Pine Flats	6,800		19	*	*	
Coldbrook	6,800		36	*	*	*
Grout Bay	6,800		23	*	*	*
Hanna Flat	7,000		88	*	*	*
Holcomb Valley	7,400		19		*	
Horse Springs	5,800		17			
Pineknot	7,000		52	*	*	*
Group Campgrounds						
Bluff Mesa	7,600	40/8				*
Boulder	7,500	40/8				*
Buttercup	7,100	40/8		*		*
Deer	7,600	40/8				*
Green Canyon	7,400	40/8				*
Gray's Peak	7,200	40/8				*
Ironwood	6,700	25/5				*
Juniper Springs	7,700	40/8		*		*
Round Valley	6,900	15/3		*		*
Siberia Creek	4,800	40				
Tanglewood	7,700	40/8				*

Notes:
Siberia Creek is accessible by trail.
Reservations required for all group camps through Big Bear Ranger District office.

For Information

Big Bear Ranger District
P.O. Box 290
North Shore Drive, Highway 38
Fawnskin, CA 92333
(714) 866-3437

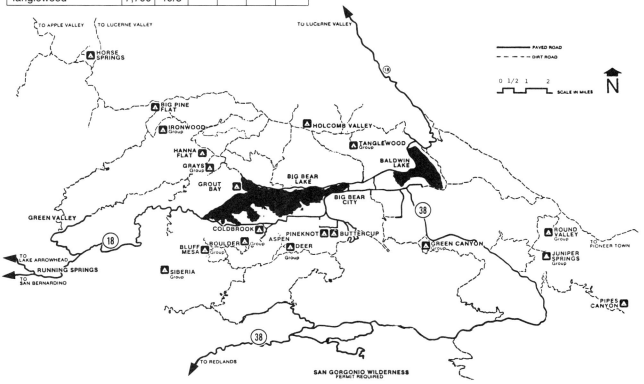

REGION 6

San Bernardino National Forest *(continued)*

San Gorgonio Ranger District

	Elevation (ft)	People/Vehicle	# of Units	Drinking Water	Trailers	Site Fee
Family Campgrounds						
Barton Flats	6,300		47	*	*	*
Heart Bar	6,900		92	*	*	*
San Gorgonio	6,500		60	*	*	*
South Fork	6,400		24	*	*	*
Group Campgrounds						
Lobo	6,600	75/15		*		*
Council	6,600	50/10		*		*
Oso	6,600	100/20		*		*
Heart Bar Equestrian	7,000	50/25		*		*
Coon Creek Cabin	8,200	40/10				*

Notes:
Heart Bar and San Gorgonio are also multi-family campgrounds. Reservations for San Gorgonio may be made at (714) 883-9044. Reservations required for all group camps may be reserved through Mistix.

For Information

San Gorgonio Ranger District
34701 Mill Creek Road
Highway 38 and Byrant Street
Mentone, CA 92359
(714) 794-1123

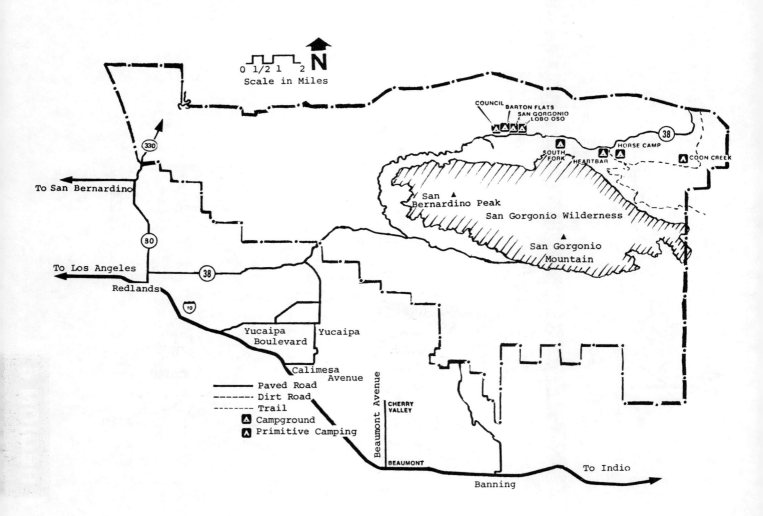

San Bernardino National Forest (continued)

San Jacinto Ranger District

	Elevation (ft)	People/Vehicle	# of Units	Drinking Water	Trailers	Site Fee
Family Campgrounds						
Boulder Basin	7,300		34	*		*
Dark Canyon	5,800		22	*	*	*
Fern Basin	6,300		22	*	*	*
Marion Mountain	6,400		24	*	*	*
Pinyon Flat	4,000		18	*	*	*
Thomas Mountain	6,800		6			
Tool Box Springs	6,500		6	*		
Group Campgrounds						
Black Mountain #1	7,500	50/16		*		*
Black Mountain #2	7,500	50/16		*		*

Notes:
Reservations for group camps are required through Mistix.

For Information

San Jacinto Ranger District
P.O. Box 518
54270 Pinecrest
Idyllwild, CA 92549
(714) 659-2117

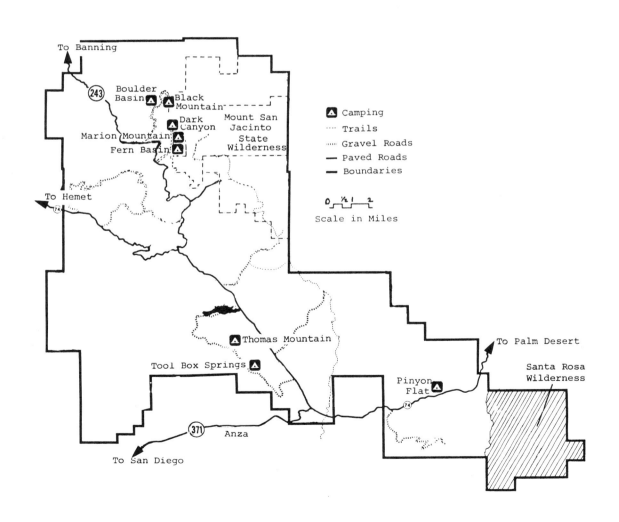

REGION 6

San Diego Coast State Beaches

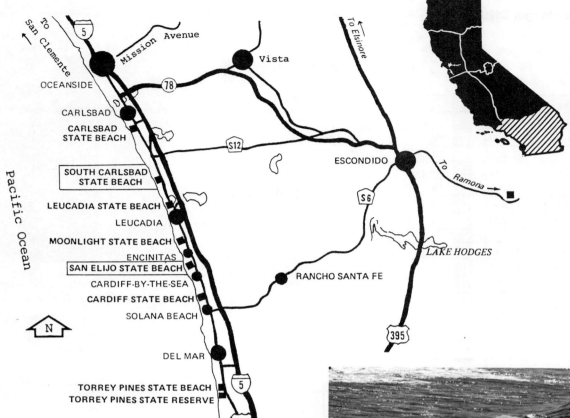

Location

The 7 state beaches just north of San Diego are among the most popular units of the State Park System. Two of these San Diego County state beaches have camping facilities. The 39-acre San Elijo State Beach is located on old Highway 101 and has 9,130 feet of ocean frontage. South Carlsbad State Beach consists of 135 acres, has 18,032 feet of ocean frontage, and is located 3 miles south of Carlsbad on Carlsbad Boulevard.

Special Notes

The campgrounds at San Elijo and at South Carlsbad are situated on bluffs overlooking the Pacific. Stairs lead from the campgrounds to the beaches. Surfing is popular at all the beaches. Please check with the lifeguards for suggestions on surfing safely. Surfers and swimmers alike should watch for riptides, denoted by brownish, swirling areas of water; if you get caught in one, *don't panic*—relax and drift with the current, swimming parallel to the shoreline and working your way in.

A surfboard is not a typical piece of camping gear for most folks, but it can be for a California camper!

San Elijo State Beach

For Information

San Elijo State Beach
2680 Carlsbad Blvd.
Carlsbad, CA 92008
(619) 237-6766

Facilities & Activities

171 developed campsites
campsites for disabled
showers
35-foot trailers; 35-foot campers/motorhomes
fishing
swimming
supplies
on State Park Reservation System (Jan.—Nov.)

It's reported that 80% of California's population lives within 30 miles of the coast—but what a coast!

South Carlsbad State Beach

For Information

South Carlsbad State Beach
2680 Carlsbad Blvd.
Carlsbad, CA 92008
(619) 438-3143

Facilities & Activities

222 developed campsites
campsites for disabled
showers
35-foot trailers; 35-foot campers/motorhomes
trailer sanitation station
fishing
swimming
supplies
on State Park Reservation System
   (mid-March—Dec.)

While some find peace and solitude in a barren desert, others find them in the crashing surf of a restless ocean.

REGION 6

San Onofre State Beach

For Information

San Onofre State Beach
3030 Avenida del Presidente
San Clemente, CA 92672
(714) 492-4872

Location

   San Onofre State Beach is located 3 miles south of
San Clemente on I-5 (Basilone Road). The 3,036-
acre state beach is in San Diego County, has 3½
miles of sandy beaches, and the camping area is at
100 feet elevation.

Facilities & Activities

221 developed sites
20 walk-in tent sites
campsites for disabled
outside cold showers
enroute campsites
group camping area (50 person/12 vehicle
   max.)—on State Park Reservation System; all
   year; developed; cold/outdoor showers; 18-foot
   max. length; primarily tent camping
fishing
hiking trails
swimming
on State Park Reservation System
   (mid-March—mid-Sept.)

Special Notes

   The abandoned highway along the bluffs above
the main beach serves as a camping area. Tent
camping is not practicable in most locations on the
blacktop road, but Echo Arch Campground, on a
terrace between the bluffs and the beach, provides
primitive walk-in campsites.
   San Onofre actually has three separate beaches.
The main beach is undeveloped and is reached by 6
main trails that have been cut into the bluffs from
the old abandoned highway that serves as day-use
parking and camping space. The San Onofre Surf
Beach at the north end has a separate access road.
This beach is known for its surfing. Trestles Beach
has no vehicle access; visitors walk in along the
beach to this isolated section at the mouth of San
Mateo Creek.

Camp Pendleton Marine Corps Base

Basilone Road

USMC Checkpoint

Interstate 5

San Clemente

San Clemente
State Beach

SAN ONOFRE SURF BEACH

ECHO ARCH HIKE-IN CAMP

PARK OFFICE ENTRANCE STATION
SAN ONOFRE STATE BEACH

TRESTLES BEACH

State Park Area

SCALE IN METERS 0   6010   1220   1830   2440
SCALE IN FEET 0   2000   4000   6000   8000

Pacific Ocean

Silver Strand State Beach

For Information

Silver Strand State Beach
5000 Highway 75
Coronado, CA 92118
(619) 435-5184

Location

Silver Strand State Beach is located 4½ miles south of Coronado on SH 75. This 428-acre San Diego County park occupies the narrow strip of land between San Diego Bay and the Pacific Ocean that connects the city of Coronado with the mainland.

Facilities & Activities

enroute campsites for self-contained RVs only at parking lot #4
showers
picnicking
fishing
swimming

If getting wet is the worst thing that can happen to you during an adventure, go for it!

Special Notes

This state beach is named for the tiny silver seashells in the sand. The park's extensive beach frontage on both the bay and the ocean, combined with the area's mild climate helps make the park one of the finest areas of its kind on the West Coast. The ocean beach facilities include 4 large parking lots accommodating nearly 1,500 cars. Three pedestrian tunnels lead from the parking lots under the highway to the bay side of the park. Here the calmer, warmer water invites swimming. The ocean side of the park is favorable for swimming, surfing, cookouts, and fishing. South of the developed area stretch 1½ miles of natural ocean beach, affording the chance for fine beachcombing.

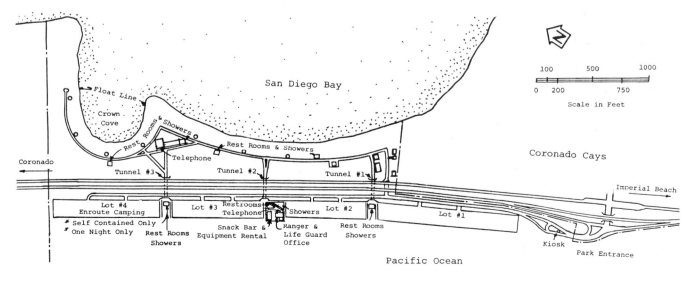

Silverwood Lake State Recreation Area

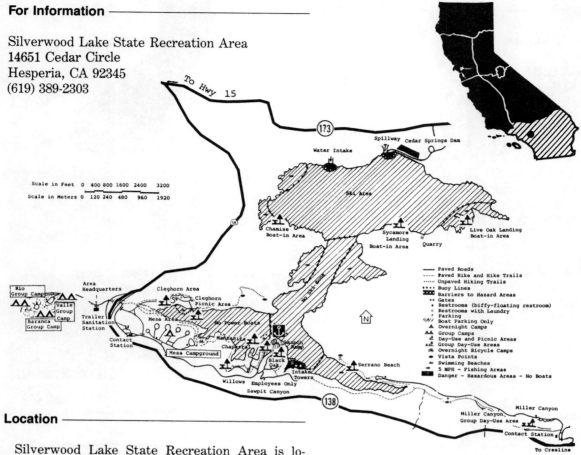

Location

Silverwood Lake State Recreation Area is located 30 miles north of San Bernardino on Highway 138. This San Diego County park, at an elevation of 3,400 feet, has 2,200 acres. The recreation area is surrounded by the San Bernardino National Forest.

Facilities & Activities

136 developed campsites
7-site bicycle camp
campsites for disabled
31-foot trailers; 34-foot campers/motorhomes
trailer sanitation station
3 group camps: Valle, Barranca, and Rio—on State Park Reservation System (March—Oct.); each with 120 person/30 vehicle max.; can be reserved together; developed; showers; limited RV parking; 31-foot max.
picnicking
Live Oak, Chamise, and Sycamore picnic areas reached only by boat
3 group picnic areas at Miller Canyon (each with 60 person/20 vehicle max.)

fishing
hiking trails (12 miles)
swimming
nature trails
bicycling
exhibits
boating (launch ramp, mooring, rentals, water skiing)
food service
supplies
on State Park Reservation System (all year)

Special Notes

Silverwood Lake, on the West Fork of the Mojave River, is formed by 249-foot Cedar Springs Dam and has a surface area of nearly 1,000 acres. The lake features trout, large-mouth bass, catfish, and bluegill planted by the California State Department of Fish and Game. An occasional bald eagle fishes the lake in winter. Windy days are common year-round.

Topanga State Park

For Information

Topanga State Park
1925 Las Virgenes
Calabasas, CA 91302
(213) 455-2465
(818) 880-0350

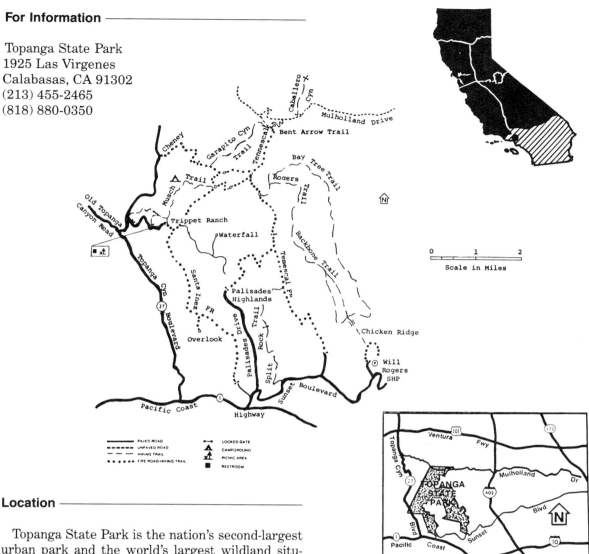

```
         0        1        2
         |————————|————————|
           Scale in Miles
```

PAVED ROAD ———   LOCKED GATE ·—•
UNPAVED ROAD ------   CAMPGROUND ▲
HIKING TRAIL – – –   PICNIC AREA ⚐
FIRE ROAD/HIKING TRAIL •••••   RESTROOM ■

Location

Topanga State Park is the nation's second-largest urban park and the world's largest wildland situated within the boundaries of a major city. Most of its 9,181 acres lie within the city limits of Los Angeles. This park is in the tan cliffs and canyons of the Santa Monica Mountains in Los Angeles County. To reach the park from Highway 101 in Woodland Hills, go south on Topanga Canyon Boulevard (Highway 27), then 7 miles to Entrada Road, then east to the park. The park can also be reached from the coastal Highway 1, via Topanga Canyon Boulevard. Elevation is 1,500 feet.

Facilities & Activities

8 sites at hike-in trail camp
1 group site for 25 persons
trail camp is 1 mile from Trippet Ranch via trail
picnicking

hiking/horseback riding trails (32 miles)
nature trails
equestrian camping (8 horses/20 riders max.);
    hitching rails; water troughs

Special Notes

A popular attraction of Topanga State Park is the Trippet Ranch self-guided nature trail, which begins at a pond, passes through open grassland, runs by a dense canopy of live oaks, and finally onto chaparral-covered slopes overlooking the ocean. In the immediate vicinity of Trippet Ranch there are numerous intersecting paths for short strolls.

Camping Equipment Checklist

The following checklists are designed to guide you in planning your next camping trip. Your needs will vary according to the type, length, and destination of your trip, as well as personal preferences, number of persons included, season of the year, and budget limitations.

Obviously, all items on the checklists aren't needed on any one trip. Since using checklists helps you think more methodically in planning, these extensive lists should serve merely as a reminder of items you may need.

When using these checklists to plan a trip, the item may be checked (✔) if it needs to be taken. Upon returning, if the item was considered unnecessary, a slash could be used: ✘. If a needed item was forgotten, a zero could be used (0); if the item has been depleted and needs to be replenished, an encircling of the check could be used; ✅. This is of particular importance if you camp regularly and keep a camping box packed with staples that can be ready to go on a moment's notice.

Cooking equipment needs are quite dependent on the menu—whether you plan to cook and eat three balanced meals a day or whether you plan to eat non-cooked meals or snacks the entire trip. Many campers find it helpful to jot down the proposed menu for each meal on a 4 × 6″ index card to help determine the grocery list as well as the equipment needed to prepare the meal. By planning this way, you'll avoid taking equipment you'll never use and you won't forget important items.

Typical Menu with Grocery and Equipment Needs

MEAL: Saturday breakfast		Number of Persons: 5
MENU	GROCERY LIST	EQUIPMENT
orange juice	Tang	camp stove
bacon	10 slices bacon	gasoline, funnel
eggs (scrambled)	8 eggs	folding oven
biscuits	1 can biscuits	frying pan
	peach jelly	baking pan
	honey	pitcher
	margarine	mixing bowl
	salt	cooking fork, spoon
	pepper	

Shelter/Sleeping:

___ Air mattresses
___ Air mattress pump
___ Cots, folding
___ Cot pads
___ Ground cloth
___ Hammock
___ Mosquito netting
___ Sleeping bag or bed roll
___ Tarps (plastic & canvas)
___ Tent
___ Tent stakes, poles, guy ropes
___ Tent repair kit
___ Whisk broom

Extra Comfort:

___ Camp stool
___ Catalytic heater
___ Folding chairs
___ Folding table
___ Fuel for lantern & heater
___ Funnel
___ Lantern
___ Mantels for lantern
___ Toilet, portable
___ Toilet chemicals
___ Toilet bags
___ Wash basin

Clothing/Personal Gear:

___ Bathing suit
___ Boots, hiking & rain
___ Cap/hat
___ Facial tissues
___ Flashlight (small), batteries
___ Jacket/windbreaker
___ Jeans/trousers
___ Pajamas

___ Pocket knife
___ Poncho
___ Prescription drugs
___ Rain suit
___ Sheath knife
___ Shirts
___ Shoes
___ Shorts
___ Socks
___ Sweat shirt/sweater
___ Thongs (for showering)
___ Toilet articles (comb, soap, shaving equipment, toothbrush, toothpaste, mirror, etc.)
___ Toilet paper
___ Towels
___ Underwear
___ Washcloth

Safety/Health:

___ First-aid kit
___ First-aid manual
___ Fire extinguisher
___ Insect bite remedy
___ Insect repellant
___ Insect spray/bomb
___ Poison ivy lotion
___ Safety pins
___ Sewing repair kit
___ Scissors
___ Snake bite kit
___ Sunburn lotion
___ Suntan cream
___ Water purifier

Optional:

___ Binoculars
___ Camera, film, tripod, light meter

___ Canteen
___ Compass
___ Fishing tackle
___ Frisbee, horseshoes, washers, etc.
___ Games for car travel & rainy day
___ Hobby equipment
___ Identification books: birds, flowers, rocks, stars, trees, etc.
___ Knapsack/day pack for hikes
___ Magnifying glass
___ Map of area
___ Notebook & pencil
___ Sunglasses

Miscellaneous:

___ Bucket/pail
___ Candles
___ Clothesline
___ Clothespins
___ Electrical extension cord
___ Flashlight (large), batteries
___ Hammer
___ Hand axe/hatchet
___ Nails
___ Newspapers
___ Pliers
___ Rope
___ Saw, bow or folding
___ Sharpening stone/file
___ Shovel
___ Tape, masking or plastic
___ Twine/cord
___ Wire
___ Work gloves

Cooking Equipment Checklist

Food Preparation/
Serving/Storing:

___ Aluminum foil
___ Bags (large & small, plastic & paper)
___ Bottle/juice can opener
___ Bowls, nested with lids for mixing, serving & storing
___ Can opener
___ Colander
___ Fork, long-handled
___ Ice chest
___ Ice pick
___ Knife, large
___ Knife, paring
___ Ladle for soups & stews
___ Measuring cup
___ Measuring spoon
___ Pancake turner
___ Potato & carrot peeler
___ Recipes
___ Rotary beater
___ Spatula
___ Spoon, large
___ Tongs
___ Towels, paper
___ Water jug
___ Wax paper/plastic wrap

Cooking:

___ Baking pans
___ Charcoal
___ Charcoal grill (hibachi or small collapsible type)
___ Charcoal lighter
___ Coffee pot
___ Cook kit, nested/pots & pans with lids
___ Fuel for stove (gasoline/kerosene/liquid propane)
___ Griddle
___ Hot pads/asbestos gloves
___ Matches
Ovens for baking:
___ Cast iron dutch oven
___ Folding oven for fuel stoves
___ Reflector oven
___ Tote oven
___ Skewers
___ Skillet with cover
___ Stove, portable
___ Toaster (folding camp type)
___ Wire grill for open fire

Eating:

___ Bowls for cereal, salad, soup
___ Cups, paper & styrofoam
___ Forks
___ Glasses, plastic
___ Knives
___ Napkins, paper
___ Pitcher, plastic
___ Plates (plastic, aluminum, paper)
___ Spoons
___ Table cloth, plastic
___ _____
___ _____

Clean-Up:

___ Detergent (Bio-degradable soap)
___ Dish pan
___ Dish rag
___ Dish towels
___ Scouring pad
___ Scouring powder
___ Sponge

Hiking/Backpacking Checklist

This list is not meant to be all inclusive or necessary for each trip. It is a guide in choosing the proper gear. Although this list was prepared for the hiker/backpacker, it is quite appropriate for anyone using the backcountry, whether they are traveling by foot, canoe, bicycle, or horse. Parentheses indicate those optional items that you may not want to carry depending upon the length of the trip, weather conditions, personal preferences, or necessity.

Ten Essentials for Any Trip:

___ Map
___ Compass
___ First aid kit
___ Pocket knife
___ Signaling device
___ Extra clothing
___ Extra food
___ Small flashlight/extra bulb & batteries
___ Fire starter/candle/waterproof matches
___ Sunglasses

Day Trip (add to the above):

___ Comfortable boots or walking shoes
___ Rain parka or 60/40 Parka

___ Day pack
___ Water bottle/canteen
___ Cup
___ Water purification tablets
___ Insect repellant
___ Sun lotion
___ Chapstick
___ Food
___ Brimmed hat
___ (Guide book)
___ Toilet paper & trowel
___ (Camera & film)
___ (Binoculars)
___ (Book)
___ Wallet & I.D.
___ Car key & coins for phone
___ Moleskin for blisters
___ Whistle

Overnight or Longer Trips
(add the following):

___ Backpack
___ Sleeping bag
___ Foam pad
___ (Tent)
___ (Bivouac cover)
___ (Ground cloth/poncho)
___ Stove
___ Extra fuel
___ Cooking Pot(s)
___ Pot scrubber
___ Spoon (knife & fork)
___ (Extra cup/bowl)
___ Extra socks
___ Extra shirt(s)
___ Extra pants/shorts
___ Extra underwear
___ Wool shirt/sweater
___ (Camp shoes)

___ Bandana
___ (Gloves)
___ (Extra water container)
___ Nylon cord
___ Extra matches
___ Soap
___ Toothbrush/powder/floss
___ Mirror
___ Medicines
___ (Snake bite kit)
___ (Notebook & pencil)
___ Licenses & permits
___ (Playing cards)
___ (Zip lock bags)
___ (Rip stop repair tape)
___ Repair kit—wire, rivets, pins, buttons, thread, needle, boot strings

INDEX